Slavery Remembered

DATE DUE

DEC 4 1984			
DEC 1 1 1995			
APR 3 0 1988			
MAY 1 1998			
APR 8 1997			
AUG 1 9 2002			
AUG 1 9 2002			
MAY 2 8 2003			

DEMCO 38-297

Reproduced from the collection of the Library of Congress

Slavery Remembered

A Record of Twentieth-Century
Slave Narratives

by
Paul D. Escott

The University of North Carolina Press
Chapel Hill

© 1979 The University of North Carolina Press
All rights reserved
Manufactured in the United States of America
Library of Congress Catalog Card Number 78-12198
Cloth edition ISBN 0-8078-1340-0
Paper edition ISBN 0-8078-1343-5

Library of Congress Cataloging in Publication Data

Escott, Paul D   1947–
    Slavery remembered.

    Bibliography: p.
    Includes index.
    1. Slavery in the United States—Condition of slaves.
    2. Slavery in the United States—Condition of slaves—
Sources.   I. Title.
E443.E82   301.44'93'0973   78-12198
ISBN 0-8078-1340-0
ISBN 0-8078-1343-5 pbk.

To Randi

Contents

Tables

Preface

A white man can't give the history of the Negro.
Charlie Moore (?) in The American Slave,
Vol. 18, Unwritten History of Slavery.

If you want Negro history you will have to get [it] from somebody who wore the shoe, and by and by from one to the other you will get a book.
Mr. Reed in The American Slave,
Vol. 18, Unwritten History of Slavery.

As a white historian, I have been painfully aware of the problem described by Charlie Moore. It is indeed presumptuous of a white scholar to attempt to reveal how black men and women felt about their enslavement, but Mr. Reed's words explain why I can feel that I have not strayed too far from the truth. Surely the words of the slaves themselves constitute the best source on the black experience of slavery, and the narratives of former slaves are the basis of this book.

Only in the last few years have historians begun to use the Federal Writers' Project Slave Narratives and similar materials gathered by researchers at Fisk University. Despite an outpouring of new books, the reinterpretation of slavery may be just beginning, for black sources provide entirely different perspectives on critical issues and basic concepts. It is an embarrassing fact that until recently historians have studied slavery almost entirely from white sources. The inevitable omissions and distortions that arise from such an approach should be apparent. How many teachers have an accurate conception of what goes on in their classrooms and what their students are thinking? How many of us truly know how friends and family members perceive us? Discovery of the truth about any historical situation depends on the availability and use of sources from a variety of perspectives. We will never have as many sources as we need from the slaves since they did not produce the ordinary volume of written records, but the slave narratives can help to fill the gap.

My purpose in writing this book is twofold. First, I want to present essential evidence from the slave narratives as effectively and systematically as I can. Through these voluminous records some of America's slaves spoke for themselves. I have tried to let the most eloquent speak through quotation while providing summaries of the information given by all. Second, I want to comment on some of the major concepts and issues developed in the study of American slavery and offer a reinterpretation based on the evidence of the narratives. I believe that the narratives give us a picture of slavery different from what we have had before. They reveal that blacks had a deeply ingrained awareness of themselves as an oppressed racial group and that this awareness reinforced their community while it guided them in their relationships with whites during slavery and Reconstruction.

I have incurred many debts in the writing of this book. The greatest is to Raymond Gavins of Duke University, who first directed me in the study of black history, and whose industry, intellectual integrity, and deep concern for his students have been a source of inspiration for me ever since. I also want to thank several friends and colleagues who read the manuscript and made many helpful suggestions—Julia Blackwelder, Jeffrey Crow, Robert Durden, and Lyman Johnson. Peter Wood also went beyond the call of duty and offered many valuable comments. The responsibility for all errors of fact or interpretation, of course, remains mine.

When time was short four colleagues at the University of

North Carolina at Charlotte made it possible for me to gain quick access to necessary materials. For their understanding and support I want to thank Amanda Harmon, Gwen Miller, Herman Norman, and Robert Rieke. I am also grateful to Dale Wheeler and Norman Innes of the UNCC computer center, who patiently answered my many questions.

A grant from the American Philosophical Society enabled me to buy the published narratives on which this book is based. I am also very grateful to the Whitney M. Young, Jr., Memorial Foundation, whose award of a fellowship allowed me to take ten months from teaching and conduct the research for this book. A summer grant supported me during the drafting of the manuscript, and I am grateful for these funds from the Foundation of the University of North Carolina at Charlotte and from the University of North Carolina.

Slavery Remembered

Introduction:
The Narratives as a Source

The primary sources for this book are slave narratives, specifically the Federal Writers' Project Slave Narratives and two collections of narratives produced by researchers at Fisk University. These represent three of the six different projects undertaken in this century to interview former slaves before their death. Aside from the published nineteenth-century narratives that have been used very effectively by John Blassingame, these narratives constitute the most important body of interviews with former slaves, and the interviews studied in this book comprise a large majority of the total.[1]

The earliest attempt to interview former slaves came at Fisk University in Tennessee in 1927. A. P. Watson, a graduate student in anthropology who worked under the guidance of Dr. Paul Radin, set out to gather the religious conversion experiences and autobiographical accounts of former slaves. After two years of careful labor, he had compiled transcripts of interviews with one hundred individuals. As Watson was completing his work, another researcher at Fisk, Mrs. Ophelia Settle Egypt of the Social Science Institute, was beginning a separate interview project. In 1929 and 1930 she contacted more than one hundred former slaves and later made thirty-seven transcripts available as "Social Science Source Documents."[2]

At Southern University in Louisiana, historian John B. Cade was also pursuing interviews in 1929. His article, "Out of the Mouths of Ex-Slaves," published in *The Journal of Negro*

History in 1935, reflects part of this work. But the records of approximately four hundred interviews conducted later with former slaves in thirteen states have never been published and no longer seem to be available. Still another collection of interviews developed with federal support under the supervision of Lawrence D. Reddick. In 1934 about 250 interviews took place in Indiana and Kentucky, and these remain in Dr. Reddick's possession.[3]

By far the largest set of interviews, however, came out of the Federal Writers' Project of the Works Progress Administration. Between 1936 and 1938 federal authorities organized teams of interviewers in seventeen states who gathered the recollections of over two thousand former slaves. The typescript of these interviews, running to more than ten thousand pages, was deposited in the Library of Congress and has been avilable on microfiche for many years. In 1972 the Greenwood Publishing Company published the typescript, plus the two Fisk projects, in nineteen volumes under the title, *The American Slave: A Composite Autobiography*. The editor, George P. Rawick, wisely refrained from editing, and as a result scholars can examine the text of the typescript with its original revisions and emendations.[4] The Virginia Federal Writers' Project had held back most of its records for the preparation of a separate book, entitled *The Negro in Virginia*; consequently, few of those interviews appeared in the federal collection. Through the vigorous detective work of Charles L. Perdue, Jr., Thomas E. Barden, and Robert K. Phillips, many of the interviews have been recovered and published, along with valuable comments on editorial changes and distortions, as *Weevils in the Wheat: Interviews with Virginia Ex-Slaves*.[5]

What are these narratives like? The two Fisk collections differ substantially. Ophelia Settle Egypt's interviews, entitled "Unwritten History of Slavery," take the form of verbal autobiographies ranging from three to seventeen typed pages. Most are several pages or more in length, however, and of consistently good quality. The conversion experiences gathered by A. P. Watson are short and focus almost entirely on religious belief; six useful autobiographies are also included in his volume. The Federal Writers' Project produced quite a variety of written interviews. Some are short, filling only a page or two, while others go into considerable depth. The typical interview might cover four or five pages. Unfortunately, a few of the "writers" employed by the Federal Writers' Project took their vocational responsibilities too seriously and used each visit to a former slave as an excuse to demonstrate their literary creativity and skills. Prose portraits of sharecroppers' cabins or flowery descriptions of trees and surroundings resulted from such interviews, which yielded little useful information. Most of the interviewers, however, realized that their purpose was to put down on paper what the former slaves had said, and they stuck to the subject.

To assist local workers in their interviewing, the national director of the Federal Writers' Project periodically sent out directives or detailed lists of suggestions. On 30 July 1937 Henry G. Alsberg dispatched a long memorandum containing several suggestions and a list of twenty categories of sample questions. Although interviewing was already well advanced in some states, Alsberg's memorandum seems to have become a model for many of the interviews. It urged state workers to "take the greatest care not to influence the point of view of the informant" and emphasized that "*all stories should be as nearly word-for-word as is possible.*" Unfortunately, many of the interviewers could have taken the first suggestion more seriously, but most sought to comply with the second. Alsberg's sample questions, which were to be used "only as a basis, a beginning," covered three main areas: conditions of life in slavery, including work, food, clothing, religion, resistance, care of the sick, and relations with one's owners; experiences during the Civil War and Reconstruction, including contact with the Union army or the Ku Klux Klan, first knowledge of freedom, school attendance, and land; and, more sketchily, later patterns of life, including family history and religious activities. Certain questions held great potential for throwing light on black attitudes and culture. For example, one question asked, "How did slaves carry news from one plantation to another?" Among the other inquiries were the following: "Did the slaves have a church on your plantation? . . . Did the slaves ever run away to the North? Why? . . . What do you think of voodoo? . . . What medicine (herbs, leaves, or roots) did the slaves use for sickness? . . . What happened on the day news came that you were free? What did your master say and do?"[6] These questions provided an underlying structure for many of the narratives and suggest the potential value of the information elicited.

But for many years reluctance to use the narratives or suspicion about their value left these sources virtually untapped. Ulrich Bonnell Phillips, one of the pioneer students of American slavery, dismissed the narratives. "The lapse of decades has impaired inevitably the memories of men," he wrote, and therefore "the asseverations of . . . aged survivors are generally unsafe even in supplement."[7] Historians discarded the explicit racism that permeated Phillips's work long before they reconsidered his attitude toward the narratives. Not until Eugene Genovese's *Roll, Jordan, Roll*, published in 1974, did a major study of slavery make extensive use of these slave sources. Widespread doubts about their value and character remain today.

There are, in fact, many problems that must be overcome in the use of the slave narratives. A common objection is that the informants were too old at the time of their interviews to give a reliable recollection of events. Memories are fallible, and in the 1930s the former slaves were recalling events of seventy or eighty years before. Yet, it is also true that the brain records and preserves the events of an individual's life and that older people often dwell more in memory than the young. Recent studies have shown that aging does not impair the recollection of the elderly, despite society's common assumption that it does. Failing health is associated with loss of memory and intellectual function at any age, but there is no necessary connection between age and memory loss. Some authorities contend that intellectual function improves with age.[8] Furthermore, it seems likely that people would remember events that took place at critical junctures in their lives. Just as individuals in modern America remember their wedding days or graduations and family births or deaths, former slaves would be able to recall the day of jubilee when freedom came or the tragic selling of a relative. It should not be exceptionally difficult for historians, who are trained in the critical use of sources, to watch for more recent attitudes that might taint the recollection of an early event or to separate common knowledge and shared impressions from the actual experiences of an individual. This author has tried to do these things and, to minimize the dangers arising from second- or third-hand testimony, has excluded from aggregations of data all events that did not occur on the slave's own plantation. Unhappily, this decision might have excluded important occurrences that a wary informant attributed to a nearby plantation, but pitfalls exist on all sides. In the end each reader will have to judge the success of the author's methods, which are explained in greater detail in Appendix A.

The most formidable problem encountered in using the narratives is the problem of candor. The Civil Rights Movement was decades beyond the horizon in the 1930s when former slaves were interviewed, and southern blacks lived in the grip of a system of segregation that was nearly as oppressive as slavery. Old, poor, and dependent, they were trying to stay alive while the nation's economy lurched sickeningly through its most serious crisis. They could not afford to alienate local white people or agents of the federal government, which might provide them with vital relief or an old-age pension. All the rules of racial etiquette had to be observed, and the informant had to give priority to appeasing his interviewer rather than telling the truth about the past. Thus some of the former slaves pulled their punches.

Reverend Ishrael Massie, for example, frankly asserted, "I ain't tellin' white folks nuthin' 'cause I'm skeer'd to make enemies," and Jennie Patterson admitted that "even now in dis new day an' time" she carefully rationed what she told white folks. Perhaps Martin Jackson described the problem most eloquently when he said, "Lots of old slaves closes the door before they tell the truth about their days of slavery. When the door is open, they tell how kind their masters was and how rosy it all was." Interviewers should have been aware of such pressures and known when the door was open, but they often were not. One white woman who called on an elderly South Carolina couple asked the wife why they had no electricity when there was current available at their door. The reply was very revealing: "White folks run me [away] if I do that!" Seeming to grasp the situation, the interviewer observed that her informants lived "with many old and odd beliefs one being that the white man only is entitled to the good things—the better things." But in her very next sentence the interviewer complacently repeated the "old and odd belief" that this elderly couple "like most old ex-slaves . . . love and revere the names and memories of their old masters."[9] Occasionally a former slave was interviewed by the grandchildren of his old master, though the circumstances of such an interview were unlikely to encourage frankness.

As a result of these coercive situations, former slaves clammed up and said little of substance. A white interviewer who signaled his traditional, racist attitudes frequently obtained only a long series of entertaining but irrelevant stories for his trouble. Blacks knew how to amuse whites, for story telling was a basic survival tactic that could be used in difficult moments. They also knew how to evade a dangerous question. The same individuals who talked at length about Abraham Lincoln generally had an astounding ignorance of the president of the Confederacy. Most, like Bert Luster, simply said, "Don't know much about Jeff Davis," and that was all they would say.[10]

It is surprising, though, how many were willing to reveal their feelings and come out into the open with their stories. "Some white folks might want to put me back in slavery if I tells how we was used in slavery time," Wes Brady told his interviewer, "but you asks me for the truth." Risks are worth taking for some purposes, and the interviews seemed very important to most of the former slaves. They wanted their story to be told; they wanted future generations to know what slavery had been like, and they were willing to risk truth telling. Accordingly, the slave narratives contain many passages of remarkable candor. As one example, take the comment of Elijah Green, who discussed the South's famed leader, John C. Calhoun: "I never did like Calhoun 'cause he hated the Negro; no man was ever hated as much as him by a group of people."[11]

Elijah Green's interviewer was black, and the presence of a number of black interviewers added greatly to the value of the narratives. In the Federal Writers' Project, several states employed at least one black interviewer, and two state projects relied upon a majority of black workers. Eight of the eleven writers who could be identified in Florida's project were black; thirteen of Virginia's twenty interviewers shared the same skin color as their informants. Black people also conducted all of the Fisk interviews. In all more than 400 of the 2358 usable interviews came from black writers.[12] Thus almost one-fifth did not take place across a steep racial barrier (see table I.1).

As might be expected, the black interviewers obtained information that white workers could not get. There was more honesty in the all-black interviews and less obeisance to social rituals. In most Federal Writers' Project narratives, even those who were harshly critical of their former masters often found something complimentary to say about them first. Racial etiquette required that the former slaves express gratitude and respect for their white folks. This ritual was wholly lacking in

Table I.1.   *Interviews Conducted by Each Race*

Race of Interviewer	Number of Interviews	Percentage
White	1239	52.5
Black	406	17.2
Other	4	0.1
Undetermined	709	30.1
Total	2358	99.9

the Fisk collections. The former slaves said very little about loving their owners when they were not in the presence of whites who expected it. Black interviewers were also more likely to learn about tricks such as adding stones to the baskets of cotton that were weighed at the end of the day. The Florida narratives contained much more information than other state collections on such topics as the slaves' interest in the Civil War, their desire to be free, the practice of slave breeding, and sexual abuse by whites. As tables I.2 through I.4 illustrate, former slaves were more likely to reveal to black interviewers than to white ones negative feelings about their treatment and masters and their willingness to act upon those feelings.

Table I.2.   *Race of Interviewer and Ratings of Food*

	Percentage	
Ratings of Food	White Interviewers (N = 506)	Black Interviewers (N = 165)
Good	72.1	46.1
Adequate	9.7	22.4
Inadequate	9.1	18.8
Bad	3.0	1.2
Same as master	6.1	11.5

Table I.3   *Race of Interviewer and Attitude toward Master*

	Percentage	
Attitude toward Master	White Interviewers (N = 795)	Black Interviewers (N = 267)
Very favorable	9.2	6.7
Favorable	64.2	52.8
Unfavorable	19.6	18.7
Very unfavorable	6.4	20.2
Ambivalent	0.6	1.5

Note: More will be said in Chapter 2 about the context of these ratings. The former slaves ranked their masters not on an absolute scale but relative to harsh slaveowners about whom they had heard. Thus, a good master typically was one who "didn't whip much."

Table I.4   *Race of Interviewer and Decision to Stay With or Leave Master at End of War*

	Percentage	
Decision	White Interviewers (N = 816)	Black Interviewers (N = 248)
Left during war	4.4	13.3
Left immediately	6.6	11.3
Left within one year	28.5	26.2
Left, time uncertain	9.9	13.3
Stayed one to five years	14.4	11.7
Stayed several years or more	25.0	15.7
Stayed, time uncertain	9.9	5.6
Left but returned	1.3	2.8

Even if one accepts the view that the interviews conducted by blacks can correct and amplify conclusions drawn from the narratives, other questions remain. How representative of the entire slave population were the people who were interviewed? If the interviews had been technically perfect but the sample badly skewed, the information obtained would still be unreliable. There are biases in the slave narratives, but they are not fatal and in some respects are less serious than many historians have thought.

The creators of the collections of slave narratives did not set out to obtain a random sample of the slave population or even of the former slaves who were still alive. In fact, they used no scientific principle of selection at all. Interviewers merely looked up elderly black people about whom they had heard and asked them to talk about their experiences. Thus a number of factors influenced the selection of an informant. A list of these, by no means exhaustive, might include the fact that the former slave was still alive, that the former slave was available on a particular day, or that he or she was known to the interviewer. The list might also note the energy of the interviewer and even the size and scope of the project in which the interviewer worked.

One of the oddities of the Federal Writers' Project was that the most extensive state project was in Arkansas, a state which had a small population and relatively few slaves in 1860. Nevertheless, because local officials proved ambitious and industrious, almost seven hundred interviews originated in that state. Obviously this large number would tend to misrepresent the experience of slavery, had those interviewed been slaves in Arkansas. In fact, they had not been. The vast majority of former slaves who were interviewed in "the land of opportunity" had moved there after the Civil War. When one looks at the location of the former slaves before emancipation, Arkansas does not dominate the Federal Writers' Project and Fisk collections. As table I.5 suggests, the locations during slavery and Reconstruction of those who were interviewed roughly approximate the locations for the entire black population. The correspondence is not exact, but the cotton states are strongly represented and border areas do not dominate. Patterns of migration during Reconstruction are reflected faithfully: the percentage of former slaves who were in older southern states like South Carolina and Georgia falls while the percentage of former slaves in new areas like Texas, Arkansas, and Kansas rises. Thus the problem of geographical distribution is not severe.

It is also possible that the interviewers reached a group of former slaves who were disproportionately prosperous or poor and that the financial condition of the former slaves at the time of their interviews affected their recollections of slavery. The vast majority of southern blacks, of course, were poor during the 1930s, and impressionistic evidence from the narratives confirms that this was the typical condition of most of those interviewed. Moreover, a comparison of attitudes and land ownership reveals little difference in viewpoint between those who owned no land and those who were more prosperous.

The occupational distribution of the informants presents a more serious defect. As various commentators have suspected, house servants are substantially overrepresented in the slave narratives. The number of informants who had no job during slavery or merely performed light chores on the plantation is also very high. The heavy weighting of former house servants probably arose from the fact that interviewers were pursuing former slaves known to them or to other white people. Because house servants often became enmeshed in the activities of their owners' families, they probably had good opportunities to maintain contact with whites through the decades following emancipation. Such contact may have been forced upon them, they may have chosen to sustain it to gain material and social advantages, or personal relationships may simply have persisted. The overrepresentation of those who did not participate in the adult slave work force, on the other hand, is purely a function of age. Most former slaves who had reached maturity before the

Table I.5   Location of Interview Compared to Location during Slavery and Reconstruction

	Percentage		
	Location of Interview *(N = 2358)*	*Location during Slavery* *(N = 2280)*	*Location during Reconstruction* *(N = 1795)*
Maryland	0.9	0.8	0.3
District of Columbia	0.0	0.0	0.1
Kentucky	1.2	4.0	2.6
Missouri	3.6	3.1	2.7
Kansas	0.1	0.0	0.2
Virginia	5.4	7.3	4.3
North Carolina	7.5	9.7	9.3
Tennessee	3.1	7.1	7.1
Arkansas	29.5	10.0	15.2
South Carolina	12.1	14.6	12.0
Georgia	7.2	11.3	10.8
Florida	2.9	1.1	1.3
Alabama	5.3	7.7	6.4
Mississippi	1.1	8.5	8.8
Louisiana	0.0	3.9	3.6
Texas	12.9	10.1	13.1
West Virginia	0.0	0.0	0.1
Ohio	1.4	0.0	0.7
Indiana	2.6	0.0	0.4
Illinois	0.0	0.0	0.2
Pennsylvania	0.0	0.1	0.1
New York	0.0	0.0	0.1
Oklahoma	3.1	0.6	0.6

Table I.6 Land Ownership and Attitude toward Master at Time of Interview

Attitude toward Master	Owns No Land (N = 15)	Owns Home Only (N = 93)	Percentage		
			Owns Home And Up To 100 Acres (N = 67)	Owns Home And More Than 100 Acres (N = 8)	Data on Land Own-ership Missing (N = 1395)
Very favorable	13.3	6.5	17.9	0.0	8.2
Favorable	60.0	64.5	50.7	62.5	60.4
Unfavorable	20.0	19.4	22.4	37.5	20.1
Very Unfavorable	6.7	8.6	9.0	0.0	10.3
Ambivalent	0.0	1.1	0.0	0.0	1.0

Civil War were dead by the 1930s. Consequently, the largest portion of those who remained had been children or youths while the peculiar institution still endured.

A closer look at the years of birth of the former slaves illuminates this problem. Almost one-fifth of the informants were less than five years old in 1865, so young that they could have had very few personal memories of slavery. Their information probably came in large part from their parents. Twenty-two percent were still so small at emancipation that they would not have entered the work force, and another 25 percent were no older than fifteen. On the other hand, 34.4 percent of the former slaves had been born before 1851, and most of these had experienced the difficulties of adult life under slavery.

Table I.7   Occupations in Slavery (N = 1608)

Occupation	Percentage
House servants	32.7
Field hands	22.0
Artisans	2.2
None or child's chores	42.1

Serious as these problems are, they do not present insuperable difficulties. In the first place it is easy to adjust and correct for possible biases. If one fears that the overrepresentation of house servants or young slaves tends to produce an erroneously favorable picture of slavery, the experiences of field hands and older slaves can be examined for comparison. Then one can base an estimate of the treatment or attitudes of all the slaves upon a weighted average constructed to reflect the true distribution of the slave population. This book will not employ such methods very often. For in the second place the potential bias that arises from overrepresentation of certain groups runs

Table I.8   *Years of Birth (N = 2259)*

Year of Birth	Percentage
Before 1851	34.4
1851–1855	25.8
1856–1860	22.7
After 1860	17.1

against the major findings of this study. Astute commentators have warned that the predominance of house servants and young slaves could produce overly fond memories of the master, of the security of slavery days, and of the relationships between whites and blacks.[13] The author has found few such memories in the narratives and many of quite a different kind. Probably most readers will find this book's statement of its conclusions strong enough without corrections for possible biases in the slave narrative collections.

Ultimately, it is greater use and examination of the slave narratives that will foster understanding of their characteristics and faith in their reliability. In large part that is what this book aims to achieve. Those who retain doubts can approach the material with an open mind and draw their own conclusions. It might also be useful to recall the comment of C. Vann Woodward: "It should be clear that these interviews with ex-slaves will have to be used with caution and discrimination. . . . The necessary precautions, however, are no more elaborate or burdensome than those required by many other types of sources [the historian] is accustomed to use."[14]

1.

Two Peoples and Two Worlds

What was it like to be a slave? Historians may never be able to answer that question fully since the men and women held in bondage in the United States left few records to tell their story. The slave narratives offer the best evidence we will ever have on the feelings and attitudes of America's slaves, and these records present a story which differs considerably from some of the best known historical studies.

Since 1959 American historians have shown a deepening interest in the psychological reality of slavery. Stanley Elkins's *Slavery: A Problem in American Institutional and Intellectual Life* painted a grim picture of the psychic emasculation of black Americans by an exploitative institution that encountered few societal barriers to its operation. Drawing on analogies to the Nazi concentration camps, Elkins's book provoked a storm of controversy and some valuable rebuttals by black scholars. The best and most thorough of these replies was John Blassingame's *The Slave Community*, which stressed the strength and mental independence that slaves could derive from their own group. Along with Peter Wood's award-winning study, *Black Majority*, Blassingame's book pointed to the importance of an Afro-American culture among the slaves. This perspective has informed almost every subsequent study, including Eugene Genovese's *Roll, Jordan, Roll*.

Possessing many strengths, Genovese's work was one of the first to make extensive use of the Federal Writers' Project Slave Narratives or the interviews conducted by researchers at Fisk University. Its overall picture of the slaves, however, differed from the predominant image found in these sources. Perhaps the underlying preconceptions of the author helped to account for this result. *Roll, Jordan, Roll* carried into a study of the slaves the provocative conceptual framework that its author had developed in his studies of the masters. With great subtlety and skill, Genovese has investigated the ways in which a ruling class could control the exploited not by force alone but through the demonstration of its prestige and the power of its influence. His study asserted the moral independence and cultural unity of the slaves, yet always emphasized more strongly the pervasive and controlling influence of the masters. "The world the slaves made" was circumscribed and profoundly limited, in Genovese's view, by the world created by the masters. The slaveholders' power allowed them to reap the benefits of "hegemony" and set the physical and mental bounds within which black resistance would have to develop. Conceptually, his study of the slaves remained in large part a study of the masters and their methods of control.

Central to Genovese's view was an emphasis on the intimacies between masters and slaves as they engaged in the common activities of plantation life in North America. Along with antagonism, slavery created "an organic relationship so complex and ambivalent that neither could express the simplest human feelings without reference to the other." Shared experiences thus bound slaves and slaveholders together despite their wishes. Paternalism reinforced these interconnections as masters developed an ideology of fatherly responsibility for their black "family" and as slaves accepted the master's definition of rules while striving to reinterpret them in their own interests. This "sense of family shaped southern culture . . . [and] brought white and black together and welded them into one people with genuine elements of affection and intimacy."[1] Complex and ambivalent though it was, slaves and masters, according to Genovese, lived in the same world on the plantation.

This book rejects that view of the mental environment of

slavery, for the narratives make clear that masters and slaves lived in different worlds, indeed. The evil of enslavement and the strength of cultural differences set these two groups apart from each other and gave the slaves a fundamental sense of themselves as an oppressed racial group. For most individuals, physical proximity only heightened the sense of mental separation that existed under slavery. This study questions many of the emphases of Genovese's interpretation. Beyond a doubt, for example, paternalism was a part of the antebellum social order in the South. Politicians and slaveholders talked about it frequently, and its tenets were widely known. But the question remains, For whom did it exist and what were its purposes? Clearly some slaveowners took paternalism seriously and strove to live up to their duties and obligations under it. But a much larger number probably felt more interest in enlarging their crops and their profits than in faithfully ministering to their slave "children." Paternalism may have existed for white southerners primarily as a defense against outside criticism and as an argument that they were giving their bondsmen all the care that they required. Paternalism related more to talk about the plantation than to what actually went on there.

For some slaves who speak in the narratives, paternalism was a reality. James Southall, formerly a slave in Tennessee, had a master who fostered self-reliance among his bondsmen and emancipated them all before the Civil War. Unlike most masters, who never intended their "children" to grow up, perhaps this man truly was "sort of father to all" of his slaves. Few of the former slaves described such owners, but some admitted that they had been awed by the position and style of the whites. As one man reported, "I thought in dem days white folks was God, didn't know no better."[2]

There were also cases of genuinely warm feeling between slaves and their masters. Although southern society decreed a rigidly subordinate place for blacks as a group, some whites chose to be friendly to certain blacks, who responded in kind to considerate treatment. In such cases the individuals involved made an exception of each other without forgetting the enmity that existed between their groups. Some former slaves testified eloquently to the feeling they had for their masters. "I was old enough," said Ezra Adams, "to know what de passin' 'way of old marster and missus meant to me. De very stream of lifeblood in me was dryin' up, it 'peared lak. When . . . missus passed 'way, . . . I 'minded myself of a little tree out dere in de woods in November. . . . I was just lak det tree wid all de leave gone, naked and friendless." Others shared the sorrows of their owners, and some "was right in de room when Ol' Marster died, an' dey cried something awful."³

The friendships that existed within slavery often developed from the intimacies of plantation life as Genovese suggested. Junius Quattlebaum explained that his master shared the festivity of a corn shucking to the point of getting drunk. The next day no one had to work because the master was hung over. This owner also joked frequently with his slaves and arranged a common Christmas celebration each year. Years later his former bondsman could say that he had had "de best folks to live and work wid [he had] ever seen or knowed. Dere is no sich kindness dese days betwixt de boss and them dat does de work." Other masters joined their slaves in the merriment of a corn shucking or the gusto of a barbeque at which "de white folks come down and eat long side de cullerd." Mandy Morrow, whose master owned only one large family of slaves and never whipped them, reported, "We all lives in one big family, 'cept us have dinin' room for de cullud folks." Another demonstration of intimacy occurred at the end of the Civil War on a small plantation in Texas, where the owner and his guests were dancing and singing. Hearing his slaves joining in from the back yard on "Massa's in de Col', Har' Ground," the master called them inside; "so we'uns goes in de house," reported one bondsman "and sings dat for de white folks and dey jines in de chorus." These expressions of common feeling clearly seem genuine, but they were not numerous. Of the other professions of love for the master that appear in the slave narratives, many represented only gestures to the expectations of a segregated society and were contradicted by the rest of the slave's story. Still others revealed the desire of hungry people for the steady meals that slavery had provided.[4]

There was no guarantee that the intimacies of plantation life would lead to friendship, and the opposite was more often the case. The context of any relationship exerts a great effect on its character, and relations of warmth and trust rarely grow where there is no mutual respect or equity. When circumstances compel people to live and work alongside each other, they will generally find some means of lessening tensions and smoothing social contacts; but their real feelings may lie deep below the surface. For black Americans the injustice of bondage was the massive fact at the center of their relationships with whites. For white southerners, whether slaveowners or not, racism set the bounds for their dealings with blacks. Such feelings precluded most possibilities for friendship. Southerners who lived on plantations had to discover some patterns of getting through the days with each other. They had to adjust to the rhythms of plantation life, and these lent a common structure to black and white experience. But intimacy on the practical level did not amount to a common outlook. The substance of the slave's feelings generally lay hidden from white eyes. Had the planters been able to see, they would have discovered anger and smoldering resentments.

Some of the former slaves revealed their awareness of condescension by whites, even in the midst of shared pleasures of plantation life. Georgia Johnson related that "Marster used to git my sister to shout [dance] for him. I kin just see her now, a-twistin' and jumpin' and hollerin' for all de world lak grownup Niggers done at meetin's and baptizin's, 'til she done fell out. Den Marster, he say, 'Take her to de kitchen and feed her good.'" For this master the Negro shout was a source of amusement; for this slave it was a source of food. But for both the relationship was fundamentally degrading and provided no basis for mutual respect. Other masters also used their slaves as a source of amusement, without the respect required to bring the groups closer together. Eliza Evans, once a slave in Alabama, recalled that once a week all the black children had to eat dinner at the big house. With sensitivity unusual for her age, she would "just sit there" until they let her go home. "I don't know why they had us up there unless it was so they could laugh at us," she explained.[5]

Another note sounded repeatedly in the narratives is suspicion of the master's motives. The essence of slavery was exploitation; consequently, to the slave kindly actions often signified not real concern but some pursuit of the master's advantage. Henry Wright's master allowed his slaves to tend gardens and sell their vegetables in the nearest town. On occasion he took the produce to town and sold it himself, returning with the money. At these times the slaves all suspected that they were being cheated. Early in 1863 the master of a Virginia slave returned home to take the man back with him into the army as a servant and horseman. As soon as this slave learned of Lincoln's Emancipation Proclamation, he "wondered whether [his] young master had taken [him] in the army to keep the Yankees from getting [him]." Such suspicions often reached their height during the Civil War, when the hopes and prayers of slaves and slaveowners conflicted sharply. On one plantation the well-treated cook contemptuously dismissed the idea that her mistress was crying over the deaths of the soldiers: "'she's doin' all dat cryin' kaze she skeered we's goin' to be sot free.'"[6]

For many there is no doubt that suspicions and resentments merged into hatred, though this feeling could generally be expressed only to a black interviewer. As an elderly woman, Minnie Fulkes fervently believed that God would punish the whites for their cruelty to blacks. While describing the whippings that her mother suffered years before, Minnie suddenly broke out with the exclamation, "Lord, Lord, I hate white people and de flood waters gwine drown some mo." Another former slave reported that in the 1850s "the white folks treated the nigger so mean that all the slaves prayed God to punish their cruel masters." When the yellow fever epidemic of 1852 came to Virginia, many Negroes regarded it as God's retribution.[7]

But whatever the intensity of the slaves' feelings, slavery itself was the element that soured blacks' relationships with whites. Whites deluded themselves in thinking that warm relationships could generally prevail when these relations had to grow out of the bitter soil of bondage. Sometimes slaves had to explain this reality to their owners. During the Civil War a slave from Tennessee who had joined the United States Army returned on furlough to visit his old mistress. She had treated him well over the years, and after greeting him warmly, she began to recall the times she had helped and nursed him. In conclusion she exclaimed, "'And now you are fighting me!'" "'No'm,'" came the reply, "'I ain't fighting you, I'm fighting to get free.'"[8] As long as slavery, an incontrovertible fact of exploitation, continued, enforced intimacy could not bridge the emotional gulf between two peoples.

To an overwhelming degree the former slaves saw their masters as men pursuing a selfish advantage. After all, slaveholders bought human flesh to make money out of it. Somewhere beneath each act of kindness lurked the element of calculation, and the slaves were adept at identifying it. Dosia Harris, who was a slave in Georgia, made a typical comment. She reckoned herself fortunate to have had a mistress who was "a might good somebody to belong to," but she gave the woman no credit for her good treatment of the slaves. The mistress "was good to us Niggers," said Dosia, "'cause she was raisin' us to wuk for her." Will Adams from Texas made a similar observation: "The Cavins allus thunk lots of their niggers and Grandma Maria say, 'Why shouldn't they—it was their money.'" To some even the giving of gifts at Christmas was a sham, for the master rarely went beyond the necessities of life. Presents of clothing amounted to nothing " 'cause he goin' to [buy] that anyhow."⁹

As producers of everything on the plantation, slaves knew that they received relatively little in return, and they resented the discrimination. When asked to describe his food, George Lewis noted, "We got corn bread an' biscuit sometimes—an' it wus sometimes too. . . . De flour dat we made de biscuits out of wus de third grade shorts." Even with relatively easygoing masters, slavery remained the expropriation of the bondsmen's labor. They knew that their toil made possible the owner's ease. To solidify the line of caste, many owners denied their slaves desirable things that came easily to hand. "Ol' Marster hunted a heap, but us never did git none of what he brought in," said Anne Maddox. Another slave elaborated on this situation: "Us cotch lots of 'possums, but mighty few of 'em us Niggers ever got a chance to eat or rabbits neither. Dey made Niggers go out and hunt 'em and de white folks et 'em. Our mouths would water for some of dat 'possum but it warn't often dey let us have none."¹⁰

In the master's eye, slaves knew, they were not human beings with rights and a soul but beasts of burden maintained to advance their owner's interests. Slaves who were treated well were happy that they received good care, but they credited their treatment not to the master's benevolence but to his pursuit of enlightened self-interest. They knew that sensible farmers of all kinds would take care of their work animals; thus images of draft animals appeared often in their narratives. Eli Coleman said his master "fed us reg'lar on good, 'stantial food, jus' like you'd tend to you hoss, if you had a real good one." A planter in Louisiana kept a solicitous eye on the small children in the slave nursery. "Lots of times he look dem over and say, 'Dat one be worth a t'ousand dollers,' or 'Dat one be a whopper.' You see, 'twas jus' like raisin' young mules." Another master put it this way: "A well-fed, healthy nigger, next to a mule, is de bes' propersition a man kin 'ves' his money in." Harre Quarls, formerly a slave in Texas, summed the situation up simply when he said, "Massa was purty good. He treated us jus' 'bout like you would a good mule."[11] Prudent owners took good care of their property, but they did not recognize its rights, and— human emotions being what they are—the master's sense of his investment was no guarantee against mistreatment.

Knowledge of the fundamental inequities in slavery led many of the former slaves to make a special effort not to give too favorable an impression of bondage. If one's owner had supplied good care and adequate food, the interviewer still needed to know that these conditions were not universal. "Massa was purty good," said Irella B. Walker, but she immediately added, "De massas dem times, some was good and some was bad, and about de most of dem was bad." Like many others who had a relatively kind master, Bert Strong felt compelled to tell of conditions elsewhere. "We is heared slaves on farms close by hollerin' when they git beat," he said. "They beat them till it a pity." This desire to fill out the picture made these slaves' stories more truthful, for, in fact, most whites believed that at least an occasional use of the lash was necessary to maintain discipline. Although Gabriel Gilbert had a master who was "a nice man" and did not whip, "all de folks round he place say he niggers ruint and spoiled,"—a common white reaction to indulgent masters.[12]

Standing up for their human dignity, some slaves who were interviewed ripped the veil away from talk about kind masters and rejected the notion that there could be any kindness in chattel slavery. "He ain't whipped me fer nothin' 'cept dat I is a nigger," spat out Clay Bobbitt. Although Bobbitt admitted that his whippings came "mostly cause [he would not] obey his [master's] orders," he vehemently denied that the master had any justification. Slavery was coercion and whippings for cause were still cruel because the master got to set the rules and define bad behavior. He whipped and the slaves were whipped. Being punished at the master's discretion was an essential part of being a slave or "a nigger." Another slave named Barbara Haywood expressed the same attitude to her questioner: "You axes iffen our white folks wus good ter us, an' I sez ter yo' dat none of de white folks wus good ter none of de niggers." Thomas Lewis put it this way: "There was no such thing as being good to slaves. Many people were better than others, but a slave belonged to his master and there was no way to get out of it."[13]

It is easier to understand the mental and emotional distance between masters and slaves if one recalls that the vast majority of planters were not the elegant and cultured lords of the manor who have come down through romantic legend. Their power to impress their slaves was far from complete because they simply were not as impressive as Genovese's work would suggest. Of course, in the South in 1860 there were some fabulously wealthy and tastefully cultured families who could afford to treat their slaves with the indulgence that comes from unquestioned security. But most planters were not of that stripe. The South in the late antebellum period was still an overwhelmingly rural and semideveloped area. Frederick Law Olmsted found that he could often ride for a whole day through virtual wilderness before he came upon the next farm or plantation.[14] Few of the whites who lived in this society had been able to obtain anything beyond a rudimentary education. Far from being polished aristocrats, most planters had the unpretentious ways of men who were struggling to get ahead and make a buck. The majority of slaveowners, one should remember, had relatively small holdings—88 percent owned fewer than twenty slaves, 72 percent fewer than 10, and a full 50 percent owned fewer than five. Even though the majority of slaves were concentrated in fewer hands only about one-fourth lived on plantations of fifty slaves or more.[15]

The slave narratives occasionally provide a graphic illustration of these facts. Some of the former slaves from Georgia, for example, mentioned the head lice that afflicted everyone on the plantation. Both lowly slaves and exalted masters often spent their free time trying to rid their scalps of the pests. Slaves from several states recounted the bouts of drunkenness that may have constituted their master's only recreation in a life of isolated farming. Jenny Procter, who grew up on a cotton plantation in Alabama, gave a good example of the narrowly commercial values that drove her master. Rather than being a man whose aristocratic, "seigneurial" values placed him outside the crass materialism of growing America, he seemed to embody those acquisitive impulses. When the driver whipped Jenny severely for taking a biscuit, this owner rebuked him with the words, " 'She can't work now for a week, she pay for several biscuits in dat time.' " Jenny added, "He sho was mad . . . ," for this beating had disarranged the tidy calculations of profit and loss that were whirring in his brain. For most planters there was always more work to be done by the slaves, and time was an enemy. Thus the race for profits resulted in most slaves working "from sun to sun." After work, said Gus Rogers, "you went to bed, 'cause you knew that old man would sure be rapping before you were ready next morning."[16]

All things considered, it should not be surprising that there was a wide chasm between the mental world of master and slave. Injustice and prejudice have divided men from each other throughout recorded history, and American racial slavery combined within itself two of the most potent forms of these evils. Slavery was probably the most naked form of unjust oppression, and racism compounded the situation with virulent prejudice. The slaves hated their bondage, and the enforced intimacies that arose from living and working with the whites usually did not lead the blacks to excuse their masters. On the contrary the former slaves often told of incidents that starkly revealed the resentment, pain, and cold fury that ran beneath the surface of life on the old plantation.

Annie Hawkins, a slave in Texas, had an extremely cruel master: "My, how we hated him! He finally killed himself drinking and I remember Old Mistress called us in to look at him in his coffin. We all marched by him slow like and I jist happened to look up and caught my sisters eye and we both jist natchelly laughed—Why shouldn't we? We was glad he was dead." The planter's wife punished these two girls for their outburst, but said Annie Hawkins, "She didn't make us sorry." One of the former slaves interviewed by researchers at Fisk University spoke freely of her cruelty to her mistress. When the old woman suffered some form of stroke, this young slave received orders to fan the patient and keep the flies away from her. Taking advantage of moments when the two were alone, the slave would strike the mistress across the face with the fan. The paralyzed woman could never tell of her treatment. "I done that woman bad," admitted the slave. "She was so mean to me." Soon the mistress died, "and all the slaves come in the house just a hollering and crying and holding their hands over their eyes, just hollering for all they could. Soon as they got outside of the house they would say, 'Old God damn son-of-a-bitch, she gone on down to hell.'" Another slave, an oft-beaten house servant, found her opportunity to "even up" with her mistress when she discovered the woman's extramarital affair. Promptly she told on the woman and then sat back to enjoy the ruckus that followed. For some masters these unpleasant truths about their slaves' feelings remained hidden until the Civil War. Then strong emotions often came out on both sides. A Louisiana slave, for example, told how his owners cried when their two sons went off to war. Sorrow on one side brought joy on the other. "It made us glad to see dem cry," he reported. "Dey made us cry so much." At the war's end, Reuben Wood's master in Alabama could barely bring himself to tell the slaves of their freedom. "He hollered and cried" after breaking the news, and, according to Reuben, "It tickled me to see him cry."[17]

For some slaves the perception of two worlds—the sense of slave's values versus master's values and identification with the former against the latter—came slowly. Oliver Bell, who was interviewed in Alabama, felt it was natural that he had thought well of his master: "Us didn't know no better. A man was growed plum' green 'fo he knew de whole worl' didn't belong to his ol' master."[18] But for most this awareness came more quickly. It often began in childhood and was cemented in the slave's consciousness as he entered the work force, came into fuller contact with his fellows, and learned more of slavery. The trials of adult life usually strengthened these feelings.

It was possible for a young slave to grow well past infancy in a naive, childish happiness, oblivious to the painful gulf between his blood relations and his master. Slave parents were forced to labor long and hard in the fields and had little time to lavish attention on their children. One former slave stated flatly that "slave women had not time for their children. They were cared for by old women who called them twice a day and fed them 'pot likker' and skimmed milk." Another informant added that "when niggers came from de fields dey warn't no frolicken. Dey jus' went to sleep." It was also true that adult slaves had to guard against careless repetition by children of adult conversation not meant for the master's ears. Accordingly, slave children were "seen an' not heard. When ole persons came 'round," said Della Harris, "Muma sent us out an' you better not be seen." Parents drew a firm line between adult and juvenile activities, for they had to be "mighty careful of de words dey let slip dey lips." As Lizzie Davis said, "De olden people never didn' allow dey children to set an hear dem talk no time." When one considers also that many masters encouraged young slaves just to eat and play so that they would grow into strong workers, it is apparent that some could grow well into childhood without grasping the full significance of slavery.[19]

Aggregated information from the narratives gives some support to this possibility. In general, slave children were allowed to grow unburdened by any duties until age five or six. Then over the next several years, depending on the owner, children had to set to work at minor chores, such as collecting wood chips for the fire, cleaning up the grounds, or later carrying water to slaves in the field. Girls particularly often drew light assignments as house servants. By age ten most children had chores to perform, and by age fifteen virtually all slaves were at work on regular tasks (see tables 1.1 and 1.2). Abundant comments from the narratives make clear that full entry into the work force usually did not occur before age ten or twelve. Limited experiences quite naturally produced limited views. Younger slaves were more likely to speak well of their food and deny that they had been whipped or abused (see tables 1.3 and 1.4). Harsh experiences in life awaited them at a later age. Consequently, slaves who had lived through only a few years in bondage might carry more favorable views of their masters through the years.

But the happy child of plantation fable was far less common than southern whites supposed. Masters and mistresses frequently misunderstood the feelings and actions of slave children. With the gift of concentration and exclusion common to children, a young slave could fasten on some detail and ignore its context. Martha Harrison, for example, loved the white bread that her mistress gave her. When the lady died, Martha burst into tears and refused to be consoled: "I just cried and cried . . . I thought when she died she carried all the white bread with her. Folks was saying, 'Look at that po' little nigger crying 'bout her Mistress,' but I wasn't crying 'bout mistress, I was crying 'cause the white bread was gone."[20] Children's emotions commonly arise from some specific event or aspect of an event and do not constitute fixed judgments on the overall situation.

Furthermore, it is clear that many children gained an early understanding of slavery, formed their basic loyalties, and became plantation-wise well before they entered the work force. Some understood their situation well enough not to tell the master about the prayers of adult slaves for freedom, and others spied on the whites. Although masters often used candy to tempt slave children to divulge information about the grownups, Jane Montgomery turned the tables. "I listened and told mammy

Table 1.1   Occupation and Age—Male Slaves (N = 760)

Occupation	Percentage			
	Born before 1851 (N = 265)	Born 1851– 1855 (N = 204)	Born 1856– 1860 (N =175)	Born after 1860 (N =116)
House servant	30.6	22.5	13.7	2.6
Field hand	52.5	28.4	7.4	0.0
Artisan or skilled worker	7.9	0.5	0.0	0.0
Child's chores	7.5	42.6	31.4	8.6
None	1.5	5.9	47.4	88.8

Table 1.2   Occupation and Age—Female Slaves (N = 799)

Occupation	Percentage			
	Born before 1851 (N = 283)	Born 1851– 1855 (N = 220)	Born 1856– 1860 (N = 193)	Born after 1860 (N = 103)
House servant	56.5	58.2	33.7	2.9
Field hand	34.6	15.0	4.7	0.0
Artisan or skilled worker	3.5	0.9	0.0	0.0
Child's chores	4.9	20.5	19.7	3.9
None	0.4	5.5	42.0	93.2

Table 1.3   Ratings of Food and Age of Slaves (N = 1005)

Ratings of Food	Percentage		
	Born before 1851 (N = 383)	Born 1851–1860 (N = 535)	Born after 1860 (N = 87)
Good	61.9	70.7	70.1
Adequate	14.4	12.1	11.5
Inadequate	14.4	9.0	11.5
Bad	1.5	2.2	3.4
Same as master	7.8	6.0	3.4

Table 1.4   Experience with Cruelty and Age of Slaves (N = 312)

Experience with Cruelty	Percentage	
	Born before 1851 (N = 173)	Born 1851–1865 (N = 139)
Whippings or beatings	67.6	56.8
Forced sex	1.7	0.0
Asserts no cruelty	19.6	36.7
Claims justified punishment only	11.0	6.5

everything I heerd," she said. "I ate right side dat old white woman on the flo'. I was a little busy-body." Susan Snow, a child during the Civil War, had absorbed so much from her environment that one day, when she heard the white children sing a song about Jefferson Davis's superiority to Lincoln, she "hopped up an' sung" a song about the way General Pope was defeating the rebels. Even children were not too young to hate whites who irritated or whipped them, as some did. Slave children were also capable of learning from what they saw. A woman named Betty Hodge observed at an early age the bitter feelings that divided masters and servants. Her mother Lucy, a house servant, failed to come as quickly as desired one day, and the mistress rebuked her by saying, " 'You getting mean, Lucy. You like your ma.' " Lucy retorted, " 'I just like you if I am mean.' " The atmosphere must have crackled with unpleasantness and rancor, and Betty surely learned from this experience.[21]

In some slave children such lessons had developed a remarkable ability to dissemble and conceal one's feelings in front of whites. When he was only five, John Brown's white playmates told him that the war was over and he was free: "I made out like I was cryin', kivered my face wid both han's an' setch [set to] a hollorin' I didn' want to leave my mistress." Elizabeth Sparks had also learned the socially appropriate response and made believe that she was overcome with tears when the newly married young mistress chose her as a servant. Actually Elizabeth was glad because, in her words, "She didn't beat."[22]

Dissimulation became a regular part of life for most slaves, young and old. At weddings slaves were asked what they thought of the new member of the white's family. "I didn't like that," commented Elijah Green, " 'cause I had to lie on myself by sayin' nice things 'bout the person en hate' the person at the same time." Harriet Robinson told a similar story about her experiences in Texas: "Whenever white folks had a baby born den all de old niggers had to come thoo the room and the master would be over 'hind the bed and he'd say, 'Here's a new little mistress or master you got to work for.' You had to say, 'Yessuh Master' and bow real low or the overseer would crack you. Them was slavery days, dog days." Some refused to act out such charades and let their hate and detestation out into the open. Others hoped for a better day to come when the slaves could enjoy "a settin' at de white folks' table, a eating off de white folks' table, and a rocking in de big rocking chair."[23]

Most had to tolerate the discontinuity between outward actions and inner feelings, all the while taking pains to guard the boundary between the black and white worlds. Usually this boundary was strictly maintained. One black orphan, who had been raised by the whites, found in her youth that her fellow slaves "wouldn't say anything before her, 'cause [she had] stayed in the house, and et in there, and slept in there." In such an atmosphere it was unlikely that interracial friendships would develop on any scale. A small number of whites and blacks found their worlds congruent enough to permit real contact: sixty-eight slaves, or about 3 percent of the total in the narrative collections, voiced clear and unqualified affection for their masters. For the vast majority, however, any warm feelings that arose carried a heavy overlay of natural resentment at injustice. Long after the Civil War, Savilla Burrell went to see her former master, who lay on his death bed. "I set by him and kept de flies off while dere," she said. As she sat her thoughts ran in this direction: "I see the lines of sorrow had plowed on dat old face and I 'membered he'd been a captain on hoss back in dat war. It come into my 'membrance de song of Moses: 'de Lord had triumphed glorily and de hoss and his rider have been throwed into de sea.'" Even as this woman kept watch beside a dying man, human sympathy had not overpowered the human desire for justice.[24]

Such feelings were at the center of life on the plantation—a life of two people and two worlds. These emotions gave the basic flavor to plantation realities, which of course involved many additional aspects of the lives of the slaves.

2.

Conditions of Life: The Slaves' Experiences on the Plantation

What did the former slaves say about the conditions of their existence on plantations throughout the South? How were they treated and what effect did factors such as the size of the plantation have on their experiences? Moreover, how much space did plantation conditions allow for family life and the development of community values? For these questions the narratives provide answers that illuminate the slaves' perspective and reveal the strength of bonds within their group.

Comparing their early years in slavery to the poverty and hunger they were facing in the 1930s, some spoke well of the food and clothing that they had been able to depend upon the master to provide. Others, not caring to discuss their feelings about enslavement, merely allowed that their masters were not too bad, that they had gotten along all right. Among those who faced the question straightforwardly, many had bitter words for painful memories. Katie Darling, like hundreds of others, recalled the cruelty of physical abuse and simply said that she had nursed children "in them bullwhip days." Another woman, speaking in the dialect of South Carolina coastal Negroes, gave direct answers to the interviewer's questions: "See um sell slabe? I see um. Dey put um on banjo table and sell um just lak chicken. Nigger ain't no more den chicken and animal, enty [isn't it so]? ... W'at I t'ink 'bout slabery? Huh—nigger git back cut in slabery time, enty?" Carter Jackson, who was a slave in both Alabama and Texas, said simply but clearly, "It was Hell"; Delia

Reproduced from the collection of the Library of Congress

Garlic suggested both the physical and psychological cruelty of slavery when she declared, "It's bad to belong to folks dat own you soul an' body. I could tell you 'bout it all day," she said, "but even den you couldn't guess de awfulness of it."[1]

When the former slaves turned to the specifics of their existence, hard work was a nearly universal lament. The vast majority emphasized that their labor had been exhausting and unremitting, directed in a systematic fashion by their master or his overseer. Slaveowners could not supervise every minute of every slave's activity and ensure that full effort was always given, but they could take steps to keep the slaves constantly busy and to use the entire work force effectively. As one woman put it, the overseer "sho did wuk de Niggers hard; he driv' 'em all de time. Dey had to go to de field long 'fore sunup, and it was way atter sundown 'fore dey could stop dat field wuk. Den dey had to hustle to finish deir night wuk in time for supper, or go to bed widout it." Another slave explained that no one had the chance to suffer "from that disease known as 'mattress fever.' " Roused long before day to prepare their breakfasts, slaves on his plantation were in the fields "before it was light enough to see clearly . . . holding their hoes and other implements—afraid to start work for fear that they would cover the cotton plants with dirt because they couldn't see clearly." Working from sun to sun was the pervasive reality, with frequent additional chores at night. Many times slaves fell onto their beds too tired to move until morning.[2]

The necessities of life, as most slaves described them, were simple but supplied in adequate quantity. Food from plantation to plantation was basically the same—cornmeal, fat pork, molasses, sometimes coffee, and, depending on the master, greens and vegetables from a garden or animals hunted in the woods. As one woman said, "It warn't nothin' fine, but it was good plain eatin' what filled you up." To enliven this monotonous diet, the slaves invented some spicy alternatives such as kush—

cornmeal seasoned with onions or peppers and cooked in a skillet. The masters usually fed young children primarily on pot liquor and on milk and cornbread mixed together. Many poured the food out into a trough and let the children eat like pigs or with wooden spoons; afterwards the trough could be rinsed off in one operation.[3]

Clothing too was plain and designed solely for function. Young slaves, both male and female, wore long cotton shirts which hung down to their knees with a slit up the side to allow movement. Later (some complained not until puberty had become embarrassingly evident) the boys got a coarse work shirt and their first pair of britches, usually made by female slaves on the plantation. Berries or nuts gave the women's dresses some color, but these too were plain and simple. Each year the slaves generally received one or two new sets of clothing for winter and summer and one new blanket. Shoes worn by southern bondsmen in the mid-nineteenth century won no popular endorsements: many former slaves complained about both brass-toed brogans and the stiff wrap-around shoes made from plantation-tanned leather.

The above items describe the general pattern. Unfortunately, not all slaves had enough to supply their physical needs. A few masters did not furnish adequate rations, despite the irrationality involved in such a course. Some of these owners did so purposely, relying on their bondsmen to steal from neighboring farms and thus save them the cost of provisions. Some masters also failed to protect their servants from the cold. John Eubanks, a slave in Kentucky, complained that blacks on his plantation "didden have much clothes" and "no shoes": "Come de wintah, it be so cold mah feet weah plumb numb mos' o' de time and many a time—when we git a chanct—we druve the hogs . . . from outin the bogs an' put ouah feet in the wahmed wet mud. . . . The skin on the bottoms and in de toes weah cracked and bleedin' mos' o' time, wit bloody scabs but de summah healed

them again." Another slave carried bitter memories of his overseer because "he wouldn't let us have no fire, matter not how
cold us had to work jes' de same."[4]

There were many other things that could make life onerous,
even for slaves who received good food and warm clothing.
Harsh rules that constricted the bounds of daily life weighed
heavily on the minds of many slaves, perhaps to a greater extent
than twentieth-century observers might think. For a few slaves
the plantation routine never included a pass to permit visiting,
parties to generate some fun, or even a visit to church. On
Mingo White's plantation the slaves could go to church, but "we
didn' git no pleasure outten it 'case we warn't allowed to talk
from de time we lef' home 'twell us got back." A common
complaint was the denial of opportunities for education. "Some
few slaves could read and write," as Elisha Doc Garey observed,
because slaveowners occasionally ignored the law and taught
a few of their bondsmen. But most masters enforced the law
strictly, and their slaves knew that "iffen we was caught lookin'
in a book we was treated same as iffen we had killed somebody."
Reacting sternly to attempts to write, some owners had the
offender's "thumbs mashed"; so many former slaves spoke of
blacks whose thumbs were cut off that this punishment was
probably more than a mere threat.[5]

Mutilation and extreme physical cruelty were not the rule
on southern plantations, but terrible abuses did occur, as the
abolitionists often charged. To the former slaves, the fact that
these outrages could take place constituted one of the strongest
indictments of slavery. In the more than two thousand narratives,
there are scores of stories that are literally horrifying. An unidentified former slave in Georgia said that his master "had a
barrel with nails drove in it that he would put you in when he
couldn't think of nothin' else mean enough to do. He would put
you in this barrel and roll it down a hill. When you got out you
would be in a bad fix, but he didn't care. Sometimes he rolled
the barrel in the river and drowned his slaves." Some owners

branded or burned their slaves as punishment, while others applied ingenious but cruel devices of torment. The "stiff knee," an iron rod held tightly against the leg by bands at the waist and ankle, effectively prevented running away, but it also sometimes "made 'em sick . . . caze dey had dem iron ban's so tight 'roun' de ankles, dat when dey tuck 'em off live things was under 'em." Belling a slave meant strapping him into a metal harness that suspended a bell out of reach above his head. Any slave who suffered this punishment knew little rest and must have endured mental agonies.[6]

Masters who owned a gin sometimes used "de screw box what dey press bales of cotton wid" as a diabolical kind of prison. They would "put em in dere en run press right down," reported John Glover, "en dey couldn' move till dey take em out in de mornin en whip em en put em to work." Prince Smith told of a similar contraption, a small sweatbox that imprisoned the slave but left him exposed to the heat of summer or the cold and damp of winter. Smith's master also employed the Bilboa, a high scaffold on which a slave had to stand for hours. "If you don' try to keep a level head, you'll fall en you will surely hurt yourself if your neck isn't broken. Most o' de time dey were put dere so dey could break dere necks." A sadistic slaveowner in North Carolina invented a torture called "little hell," which surely was one of the worst described in the narratives. "He dug a pit just like a barbecue pit, and he would burn coals just like you was goin' to barbecue. Then he put sticks across the top and when any of his niggers didn't do right, he laid em across that pit." Men like that master were probably sick or psychotic, and such individuals did not always stop at painful tortures. Two slaves from an area near Marion, South Carolina, knew of a burying ground in the woods for murdered slaves. Many narratives tell of bondsmen who did not survive their punishment, and Jake Terriell reported that on his plantation when "a slave git leg broke . . . massa say he no more 'count and finish him up with de club."[7]

By far the most universal complaint, and the one most representative of the slave's lot, concerned whippings or beatings. In 688 narratives (almost one-third of the 2358 studied) the interviewer touched on this topic. Only 34 of these former slaves (less than 5 percent) asserted that there had been no whipping or physical abuse on their plantation. In contrast, 654 discussed various instances of cruel treatment. Both traditional white sources and the narratives suggest that whipping of slaves was common practice, used almost universally for punishment and discipline. As a white South Carolinian explained blandly to a northern journalist at the close of the Civil War, Negroes "can't be governed except with the whip. Now on my plantation there wasn't much whipping, say once a fortnight; but the Negroes knew they would be whipped if they didn't behave themselves, and the fear of the lash kept them in good order."[8] Since slavery was coercion, this practice was typical, but the slaves never ceased to resent whipping. It loomed so large in their minds that they used it as the basic reference point for evaluating masters. When the former slaves cited a reason for their opinion of the master, they focused on whipping, or its absence, two-thirds of the time. A good owner was one who did not "whip too much"; a bad owner "whipped you till he'd bloodied you and blistered you."[9]

The latter type of master could create a terrifying situation on his plantation. Essex Henry had a sadistic owner who used to take a jug of whiskey, tie up three of his slaves, and have a "whippin' frolic," drinking and beating them over a long period of time. Another slaveowner who plied the lash "till he got tired" usually "whipped them all . . . whenever [he] got mad at any of the niggers on the place." To add painful refinement to this cruelty, some master cut open the blisters on a slave's back, dripped sealing wax into them, poured a solution of fiery peppers onto the sores, or aggravated the lacerations by striking them with a hand saw. Suspending a slave on tiptoe during and after the beating increased the pain, and some masters whipped pregnant women after making them "lie face down in a specially dug depression in the ground." Quite often in any of these situations all the slaves were made to watch when one was whipped, and the terror of punishment surpassed its incidence for the individual.[10]

Southern planters were not all monsters; surely only a small percentage of mentally unstable slaveowners derived twisted pleasure from abusing their workers. But the planters were men, and they shared one of the most common and regrettable deficiencies of human nature. Rather than examining the moral issues posed by daily life, they simply followed the standards of their group and accepted practices as they found them. The mores of southern society sanctioned physical abuse of "niggers," and most white men who grew up in that society followed its ground rules. Though the slaves hated whipping and condemned its injustice, it seems clear that most masters relied on the lash, at least occasionally. As tables 2.1 and 2.2 show, a fair proportion of those interviewed for the slave narrative collections had been lucky enough to escape a personal encounter with the whip, most likely due to their youth, but only a few had lived on plantations where such punishment was unknown. Probably the large majority of southern planters whipped their slaves at one time or another.

As the tables also suggest, there were abuses worse than

Table 2.1   Reported Experiences of Cruel Treatment (N = 331)

Cruel Treatment	Percentage
Whippings	60.1
Forced sex	1.2
Other	3.0
Asserts no cruelty	27.2
Claims justified punishment only	8.5

Table 2.2   Reports on Cruel Treatment of Others on Plantation (N = 688)

Cruel Treatment	Percentage
Whippings	61.3
Sales	8.0
Murder	6.5
Forced Sex	5.8
Slave breeding	4.1
Miscegenation	2.5
Other	4.5
Asserts no cruelty	4.9
Claims justified punishment only	2.3

Note: Each report of multiple cruelties is counted here only once, giving priority to murder, forced sex, slave breeding, and sales, in that order. In the case of these more severe abuses, whipping usually took place on the plantation as well.

whipping—abuses which caused much greater mental anguish because they disrupted the private lives of bondsmen. In a variety of ways masters interfered with the sexual activities of their slaves. At one end of the spectrum, virtually all masters recognized the value of a high reproductive rate and encouraged their slaves to have large families. Fertile females, sometimes called "breed women" by the former slaves, often received special treatment—light work, good food, and a welcome period for rest and convalescence. The barren ran the risk of being sold, for as an Alabama slave put it, "Iffen she ain't er good multiplier dey gwine ter git shut er her rail [real] soon."[11]

For a much smaller number of planters, interference took more direct forms. Some supervised the pairings among their slaves and encouraged or even required a "fine and stout" man to marry a similarly built woman. In later years these forced marriages frequently broke up with the end of slavery. On other plantations, especially small holdings with an excess of women, the master used a "stockman," "travelin' nigger," or a "breedin' nigger." "Durin' slavery there were stockmen," explained Maggie Stenhouse. "They was weighed and tested. A man would rent the stockman and put him in a room with some young women he wanted to raise children from." Detailing the financial arrangements involved, another slave said that the owners of the male slave "charged a fee of one out of every four offspring for his services." The "breedin' nigger" could be from the same plantation and simply have access to more than one woman, or the master might reward "de big man" or an especially valuable hand on the plantation with more than one wife in hopes of raising "some fine, portly children." A slave from North Carolina described systematic castration, saying that for "little runty niggers . . . dey operate on dem lak dey does de male hog so's dat dey can't have no little runty chilluns." Table 2.3 enumerates the types of slave breeding reported in the narratives. Rare though such practices were, mere numbers cannot suggest the suffering and degradation they caused,[12] and it is likely that reticence caused some underreporting.

Table 2.3   Types of Slave Breeding

Types of Breeding	Frequency
Master directed pairings on his plantation	36
Master influenced pairings on his plantation	2
Master rewarded fertility or sold the barren	17
Master used a man to impregnate through visiting or polygamy	16
Master rented a man (or men) from another plantation	7
Other methods	2
Total	80

Forced interracial sex was much more frequent, according to both white and black sources. It was a highly placed South Carolina lady, Mary Boykin Chesnut, who described plantations as "brothels" and said, "We live surrounded by prostitutes." She blamed the situation on the white men, and many former slaves concurred in her assessment. Jacob Manson, for example, asserted that "at dat time it wus a hard job to find a master dat didn't have women 'mong his slaves. Dat wus a ginerel thing 'mong de slave owners." Some perverse individuals made slave men yield their place in bed and gave friends access to the women on the plantation. Although no one will ever be able to quantify the amount of interracial sex in the Old South, it is apparent that it occurred often enough to produce substantial numbers of mulatto children. America's slave population had intermarried with Indians more commonly than is often recognized, but the former slaves reported far more instances of race mixing with whites. Of course, some white-black liaisons involved real affection or pursuit of status or advantage by the slave. As a woman told the researchers from Fisk University, "Some did it because they wanted to." But coercion lay at the bottom of most instances. This same informant added, "They had a horror of going to Mississippi and they would do anything to keep from it."[13]

In the face of all these difficulties, questions naturally arise about the viability of the slave family. Forced sex, interracial relationships, and the total authority of the master all threatened the black family, but the most serious danger was the separation of established family groups, due primarily to sales. Roughly one-fifth of the former slaves interviewed for the narratives had experienced at least partial breakup of their families during slavery. Table 2.6 details the cause of these family tragedies, which involved the loss of one or more members of the nuclear family except in the single category relating to the extended family. The high frequency of family disruption reported by the former slaves is all the more striking when one considers that these

Table 2.4   Race of Father (N = 1729)

Racial Background	Percentage
Black	84.4
White	6.0
Mixed with white	3.4
Free black	2.1
Indian	1.2
Mixed with Indian	1.6
African	1.0
West Indian	0.1
Other nonblack	0.3

Table 2.5   Race of Mother (N = 1959)

Racial Background	Percentage
Black	90.8
White	0.5
Mixed with white	2.9
Free black	1.2
Indian	0.8
Mixed with Indian	3.0
African	0.6
West Indian	0.1
Other nonblack	0.2

statistics as a rule cover only the experience of children while they were growing up. Had the former slaves been older at emancipation, more of them would have lived into adulthood as slaves, and thus, with longer experience of bondage, would likely have reported higher percentages of broken families.

Nevertheless, the narratives make clear that families were a vital institution and a towering source of strength for the slaves.

Table 2.6   Causes of Family Disruption (N = 499; 21.2% of Total)

Cause of Disruption	Percentage
Sale	58.5
Gift	9.4
Move by owner	5.2
Division of estate	2.0
Broken but nearby	3.4
Otherwise broken[a]	6.4
Extended family broken	15.0

[a] A surprising number of former slaves recalled fears of having a family member stolen by slave traders. See, for example, George P. Rawick, ed., *The American Slave*, 7:Oklahoma, 296.

They refused to permit callous treatment to strip them of their humanity or obliterate the bonds that, more than anything else, give meaning to people's lives. The slaves relied heavily on their family ties in order to combat the hostile forces that tugged at the foundations of personal survival. Threatened with destruction, slave families grew closer together. An abundance of testimony detailed the devotion that husbands and wives and fathers, mothers, children, and grandparents felt for each other, while only a few former slaves suggested that family life had lost its meaning.[14]

A woman who had married only once in a long life exemplified the values of the slaves when she said of her husband, "He was the first one and the best one and the last one." Like this woman, most slaves committed themselves unreservedly to a marriage partner who could share life's trials and help to build life's joys. Few had anything better than a broomstick wedding —a ceremony based on jumping over a broomstick—and, as Collie Williams admitted, that "wasn't much"; nevertheless "dey stuck lots closer den." Echoing her judgment, other former slaves gave reports like these:

When folkses got married den dey was a-thinkin' 'bout makin' sho' 'nough homes for deyselfs, and gittin' married meant somepin sort of holy.

Marriage in those days was looked upon as something very solemn, and it was mighty seldom that anybody ever heard of a married couple trying to get separated.

When I was young . . . young folks took their time and went together a long time and [when] they married they stayed married.

Many former slaves spoke respectfully of the love that had held their parents close together throughout life and indicated that as children they had tried to replicate that devotion and give it to their parents. One child, whose mother suffered whippings from the overseer, prayed to God "dat someday he'd open a way fur me to protect mother. . . . I know if de War hadn't ended I'd [killed dat man]."[15]

Not only do the narratives contain assertions about the strength of family ties, but they give numerous poignant examples of the ways in which these bonds operated. Slaves often went to great lengths to keep their families intact. When Nettie Henry's master gave her, her mother, and her siblings to a daughter who moved from Livingston, Alabama, to Meridian, Mississippi, Nettie's father refused to accept the breakup of his family. For five years he traveled across the state line to see them. His owners carried him to Texas during the Civil War, but afterwards he returned to set up a farm for his loved ones. In another family separated by one master's decision to move, the father, who had been left behind in Mississippi, ran away, traveled to Texas, and convinced the owner of his wife and children to purchase him so that the family could be reunited. When a Tennessee slaveowner, tempted by the high price offered for a skilled blacksmith, sold this man, his family raised such a cry that the master relented, pursued the purchasers, and bought the blacksmith back. Former slaves testified that even temporary separations were painful to the close-knit families on the plantation.[16]

The cataclysm of the Civil War separated many families, but

it also provided the long-awaited opportunity for slaves to reunite with parents, spouses, or children whom they had missed for many years. The end of the war signaled the beginning of a great search all over the South for missing family members. Many slaves were like Bryant Huff's father, who when sold away had "told his wife to wait for him to return, whether it be months or years. She grieved over his departure and refused, although urged, to marry again." A few months before the end of the war, this slave found his way back to his family. Others who could not get free until the surrender set out immediately on foot and searched great distances for those they loved.[17]

Another indication of the slaves' efforts to maintain their families was their method of choosing surnames. Though whites identified slaves in terms of their master, the bondsmen generally chose surnames that would link the different generations of their families. At some point these names may have been taken from a white owner as a way of identifying the location of the family group, but many slaves, probably the majority, regarded themselves as having a name different from their master's. The former slaves reported that their family names usually followed their fathers', and if the father had a different master or already bore a family name other than his owner's, his children viewed that name as their own. This practice was not universal, but it was sufficiently widespread that the former slaves sometimes took pains to explain departures from the rule. For example, Thomas Cole said, "I was sposed to take my father's name," but due to bitter feelings between the two, "I jes' taken my old massa's name."[18] Table 2.7 summarizes the reported extent of family names adopted by the slaves and illustrates the rule that wives took their husband's name.

In slavery all marriages were not the same. "There were two kinds . . . ," explained one of the Fisk informants. "One was marrying at home and the other was called marrying abroad." Those who married abroad chose spouses who lived on a different plantation. In the slave narratives, taken together, 27.5 per-

Table 2.7   *Source of Names*

Source of Names for Male and Female Slaves and Former Slaves	Number	Percentage
Family's name, not master's	338	16.6
Not master's, unspecified	525	25.8
Follows husband's	676	33.2
Same as master's	429	21.1
Same as earlier master's	33	1.6
Invented by slave	20	1.0
Other	15	0.6
Total	2036	99.9

Source of Maiden Names of Women	Number	Percentage
Family's name, not master's	149	46.4
Same as master's	164	51.5
Same as earlier master's	8	2.5
Total	321	100.0

cent of the reported marriages were of this latter type. A variety of reasons accounted for the decision to marry away from home. Perhaps some, as John Blassingame has suggested, wanted to insulate their family life from the supervision of the master and keep their children from seeing their father whipped. But slavery's reach was so unavoidable and the slave family had developed such resilience that more ordinary explanations probably suffice. Most bondsmen, after all, did not live on large plantations; so for any individual the number of marriageable prospects could be quite limited. As Andy Marion put it, the slave might not "see one on de place to suit [him] and chances was [he] didn't suit them." The Afro-American culture's ban on marriage between cousins, which Herbert Gutman has recently demonstrated, could also have contributed to the need to look abroad. And Cupid's unpredictable nature came into play for men like Peter Clifton. "Dere was sumpin' 'bout dat gal, dat day I meets her," he said, "dat just 'tracted me to her lak a fly will sail 'round and light on a 'lasses pitcher. I kept de Ashford road hot 'til I got her."[19]

Marrying abroad entailed special problems of its own, about which some complained. "It was a hell of a way!" exclaimed one former slave, citing the added burden of getting passes to travel and winning the consent of another master. It was also possible that "a man dat had a wife off de place, see little peace and happiness . . . [if] jealousy kep' him 'stracted" when he could not be with his wife. But in most cases it seems that the separation involved in marrying abroad only heightened the joy of those times spent together. Husbands visited as often as they could—depending on the distance, generally once or twice each week—and these visits were special times for the family. Sarah Locke recalled that her father, who lived seven miles away, came to visit each Wednesday and Saturday night, and her mother always fixed "big dinners" to welcome him and celebrate. Holidays like Christmas were also joyous times, "'cause husbands is comin' home an' families is gittin' 'nunited agin." Apparently the marriages abroad were generally as successful as those on the same plantation and inspired similar devotion. For example, Adrianna Kern told of a man who used to carry his dinner three or four miles and give it to his wife, since her master did not supply enough to eat. Other former slaves told of husbands who raced the patrollers in order to see their families, and of wives who would never pay any attention to other men near at hand.[20]

On the subject of attitudes toward illegitimate children, the narratives unfortunately are of little help. One man agreed with Herbert Gutman's finding that the slave community did not look down upon an unwed mother, but the vast majority of interviews avoided the topic. Quite a few suggested, however, that the young had little knowledge of sex and that the environment in which they grew up guarded this information to a surprising extent. Liza Reynolds laughed to recall that as a young girl she had worked "all one day and a half in a hollow stump trying to find me a baby." Other women claimed that they had been totally ignorant of the facts of life until they married.[21]

If this suggestion is reliable, it would square with far more extensive evidence on the carefully supervised nature of courtship. "Dem's moral times," said Amos Lincoln, and others confirmed that courting was as much a matter of gaining the parents' approval as of winning the girl's heart. While Peter Clifton was keeping the Ashford road hot, he was also practicing the arts of diplomacy on his sweetheart's mother and father. "I had to ask her old folks for her befo' she consent," he explained. "Dis took 'bout six months. Everything had to be regular." As another informant pointed out, "A young man courted the girl in the presence of the parents. . . . When he left, the mother would go to the door with him." Despite the impediments of slavery, parental authority over the young obviously extended quite far.[22] Another social rule that was carefully observed dictated that men wait longer to marry than women. Tables 2.8 and 2.9 suggest this pattern, and further analysis revealed that the men who married in slavery averaged 22.4 years of age while the women averaged 17.6 years. Data to be presented in chapter 7 establishes the same pattern in regard to those who married after freedom.

To this point, the discussion of conditions of life has focused primarily on the perspectives and experiences of individuals. By turning the analysis toward a comparison of slavery in various settings, one can gain a broader view of what slaves' lives were like. For many years scholars have suggested that the lives of slaves were very different on small plantations as opposed to large and that the different treatment received in these settings bred correspondingly varied attitudes. The small plantation, because of its relative poverty and greater equality in the performance of agricultural tasks, supposedly engendered a closer

Table 2.8 Age and Marital Status in Slavery—Males (N = 834)

	Percentage	
Marital Status	Born before 1851 (N = 232)	Born 1851 or Later (N = 602)
Married	13.8	0.0
Unmarried	86.2	100.0

Table 2.9 Age and Marital Status in Slavery—Females (N = 826)

	Percentage	
Marital Status	Born before 1851 (N = 230)	Born 1851 or Later (N = 596)
Married	33.5	0.0
Unmarried	66.5	100.0

feeling between master and slave, while the large plantation took on the impersonality and harshness of a factory in the field. Individual examples have often been cited to support these hypotheses.

The data in the slave narratives provide only modest support for these views. As the former slaves saw it, there were marginal but not striking differences in treatment on large and small plantations. Life was not primarily good in one setting and bad in the other; for on all the plantations blacks were still slaves, and their masters worked within rather than against the system. The slaves' reports do suggest a difference in style of life, or a variation in the tone of slavery from large plantations to small.

As table 2.10 illustrates, the great majority of masters on all plantations relied upon whipping or other forms of coercion to control the actions of their bondsmen. The only difference that appears is that a portion of the masters who had fifteen slaves or less had either limited or eliminated whipping or other cruelty, while virtually all masters on larger plantations relied on force. This contrast represents a shading in favor of conditions on the small plantation, but hardly a major shift. Similarly, as table 2.11 demonstrates, slaves from small, medium, and large plantations complained with virtually the same frequency about the quality of their food, and most thought the food was good or adequate. Only on the small plantations did any noticeable proportion of bondsmen receive the same food as the master. Life there was a little, though not radically, different.[23]

These variations reproduce themselves, as one might expect, in the attitudes of the former slaves toward their master (see table 2.12). Since treatment was a little better on small planta- tions than on large, the attitudes of slaves who lived on the small plantations are slightly more favorable. Probably those who belonged to small slaveowners did enjoy somewhat more respect for their individuality and experienced fewer of the extremes of inhumanity, while slaves on large plantations tended to represent only the source of labor for a master who did not know them and was determined to achieve results. In tables 2.10 through 2.12, however, the association between the size of the plantation and the kinds of treatment or attitudes is fairly modest, statistically speaking.

Similar shadings in life conditions appeared in relation to possession of money by the slaves. The typical slave had no money to speak of and lived in a society that afforded him few opportunities for its use. In a number of cases former slaves reacted with surprise when asked if they had owned any money under bondage. "Money! No Ma'am!" exclaimed one informant, while another answered, "Lord, no sir, I never saw no money. What I want wid it anyhow?" Yet many slaves had a small amount of cash, and a privileged few were able to amass sub-

Table 2.10   Size of Plantation and Reports on Cruel Treatment of Others (Gamma = −0.58)

Size of Plantation	Percentage			
	Reports Whipping or Other Cruelty	Claims Justified Punishment Only	Asserts No Cruelty	Number
1–15 Slaves	78.9	14.0	7.0	57
16–100 Slaves	92.7	4.4	2.9	383
Over 100 Slaves	97.9	2.1	0.0	96
Total				536

Table 2.11   Size of Plantation and Ratings of Food (Gamma = 0.28)

Size of Plantation	Percentage			
	Food Rated Same as Master's	Food Rated Good or Adequate	Food Rated Inadequate or Bad	Number
1–15 Slaves	22.6	64.2	13.1	137
16–100 Slaves	3.7	84.3	12.2	570
Over 100 Slaves	3.4	82.4	14.2	119
Total				826

Table 2.12   Size of Plantation and Attitude toward Master
(Gamma = 0.21)

| Size of Plantation | Percentage | | | Number |
	Attitude Favorable	Attitude Unfavorable	Attitude Ambivalent	
1–15 Slaves	77.3	21.6	1.0	194
16–100 Slaves	68.0	30.8	1.3	796
Over 100 Slaves	60.4	38.9	0.7	149
Total				1139

Note: Here again the expressed attitudes toward the master represented relative judgments, comparisons of that master with other slaveowners. Favorable ratings were not absolute, unqualified endorsements.

stantial sums. One former slave's father, a "first-class" blacksmith, received permission to keep all money that he earned through evening work. Before slavery ended this man had saved fifteen hundred dollars.[24] There were some modest differences in possession of money that were related to the size of one's plantation. Slaves who lived on small plantations were more likely to have some contact with money, but chances of having savings were slightly better on large slaveholdings. In regard to the source of cash, the raising and sale of garden crops apparently was more common on the larger units, while slaves on small plantations were more likely to hire themselves out in their spare time to obtain a little income.

Along with the contrasts between large and small plantations, historians have often assumed that the nature of slavery varied from the old settled areas in the upper or border South to the expanding new cotton areas along the Gulf of Mexico. Impressionistic evidence from the narratives lends some support to this view, for the slaves generally believed that work was unrelenting and its pace more intense "down there" in Mississippi or other cotton states. Surely other differences existed, but, except for the expected fact that more sales were reported from the border South, the narratives shed little light on regional variations (see table 2.13).

Another notion about which the narratives can give no final proof is the idea that female slaveowners treated their slaves differently and with more consideration than male owners. There is, indeed, abundant evidence that owning slaves constituted a problem for southern women but was not perceived as a problem by southern men. Perhaps white women who had to deal with slavery adopted a sympathetic approach to their slaves. Table 2.14, which shows that the former slaves had very favorable attitudes toward female masters more often than toward male owners, tends to support this possibility, but the social pressure to speak well of white women could have skewed the

Table 2.13 Location of Plantation and Reports on Cruel Treatment of Others (N = 397)

	Percentage	
Cruel Treatment	Border South[a] (N = 167)	Gulf South[b] (N = 230)
Whippings	60.5	62.2
Sales	11.4	6.1
Murder	6.6	7.4
Forced sex	5.4	4.3
Slave breeding	4.8	5.1
Miscegenation	4.2	0.9
Other	2.4	5.7
Asserts no cruelty	4.2	5.7
Claims justified punishment only	0.6	2.6

[a]Maryland, Kentucky, Virginia, North Carolina
[b]Alabama, Mississippi, Louisiana, Texas

Table 2.14 *Sex of Master and Attitude toward Master (N = 1558)*

Attitude toward Master	Percentage	
	Male Master (N = 1448)	Female Master (N = 110)
Very favorable	7.6	19.1
Favorable	61.3	47.3
Unfavorable	20.0	24.5
Very unfavorable	9.9	9.1
Ambivalent	1.1	0.0

results. Furthermore, when the former slaves described a difference in attitude between master and mistress, the woman was just as likely as the man to assume the harsher role rather than the more sympathetic one.

In yet another highly important area—the question of class consciousness and class divisions among the slaves—the narratives are extremely informative. Whites have long believed that class lines were very strong among the slaves and that the privileged house servants identified with their aristocratic masters rather than with the common field hands. Extensive material in the slave narratives reveals that for a small minority of slaves, this view was partially correct, but that for the large majority, there was no well-developed class system and group loyalty overrode tendencies toward class divisions.

A few former slaves, primarily from the large plantations, testified that there was a fully elaborated class system among the bondsmen. Rosa Starke, who claimed that her master owned one thousand slaves on nineteen different plantations, enumerated six different social classes, ranging from two different types of house servants through artisans to three categories of agricultural workers. Her typology seemed to be based on proximity to the master and cleanliness of work, and she asserted that slaves rarely breached class lines. "A house nigger man might swoop down and mate wid a field hand's good lookin' daughter, now and then, for pure love of her," she allowed, "but you never see a house gal lower herself by marryin' and matin' wid a common field-hand nigger." Other former slaves reported that "de house servants put on more airs than de white folks" and sometimes demanded formal courtesies and signs of respect from the others. As a result "dere was no good feelin's 'twixt field hands and house servants," according to another.[25]

On large plantations, which had well-defined categories of work, there were some practical bases for ill feelings between house servants and field hands. The former, since they worked around the whites and prepared their meals, had an opportunity to receive or take better food. "If you didn't get better rations and things to eat in de house, it was your own fault, I tells you!" said Mary Raines. Furthermore, since their work put them constantly around the master and his family and guests, house servants enjoyed additional privileges of style and dress. Wash Ingram envied those who worked around the house because they "et at tables with plates" while he and the other field hands were "fed jus' like hosses at a big, long wooden trough." Others spoke of the fine clothes and higher prestige associated with house work. One carriage driver, who evidently appreciated his livery, boasted that he "was 'bout the mos' dudish nigger in them parts."[26]

Such differences could breed suspicions and hostility. If house servants truly did "hold that dey is uh step better den de field niggers," it was only natural for the field hands to resent that attitude. Ed McCree, on whose plantation the privileged servants had feather mattresses and pillows, asserted that "dem other Niggers" out of envy "slip[ped] 'round and cut dem feather beds and pillows open jus' to see de feathers fly." Another slave reported that her owners had been so successful at engendering divisions among the slaves that "you would always find one that would be tattling and would have the white folks pecking on you."[27]

These class differences appeared with considerable regularity in the marriage patterns of the slaves, according to data in the slave narratives. Because most of the former slaves themselves did not marry until after emancipation, and since many of them did not furnish complete information on their parents, the number of cases is small. Table 2.15 shows, however, that a strong tendency for house servants and skilled slaves to marry others of their occupational category existed, at least when the marriage partners lived on the same plantation. Very few house servants married field hands, and the value of Yule's Q indicates a strong relationship.[28] Under slightly different circumstances, however, these class walls could be breached in marriage. As Table 2.16 illustrates, it was considerably easier for field hands to marry house servants or skilled slaves when the couple had different masters and came from separate plantations. This suggests that the sense of class was not pervasive. Probably at least part of the tendency for marriage to take place within occupations arose from the simple fact that house servants spent most of their time with other house servants and got to know them best.

Table 2.15 *Occupations of Marriage Partners Who Lived on the Same Plantation (Yule's Q = 0.805)*

Husband's Occupation \ Wife's Occupation	House or Skilled Servant	Field Hand	Number
House or skilled servant	82.0%	18.0%	100
Field hand	33.3%	66.7%	96
Total			196

Table 2.16   Occupations of Marriage Partners Who Lived on Different Plantations (Yule's Q = 0.249)

Husband's Occupation / Wife's Occupation	House or Skilled Servant	Field Hand	Number
House or skilled servant	77.8%	22.2%	27
Field hand	46.7%	53.3%	30
Total			57

It seems certain that different kinds of work entailed different pressures and patterns of interaction with whites and therefore produced varying perspectives. House servants enjoyed or endured, depending on the individual, a highly intimate, continual association with the master and his family. House servants' work required that they develop techniques for associating with whites on terms of familiarity. It gave them a sure grasp of the bounds of acceptable behavior and the ways to bend rules. Thus, the house servant sustained a loss in privacy but gained some effective tools for personal infighting and influence. Field hands, by contrast, came less under the master's sway since he demanded only their labor. Their thoughts could be their own, but their time belonged to the master or overseer. Thus, field hands had to take their resistance into the open. The boundaries of plantation regulations were more sharply delineated in their eyes, and their relationship with the master had fewer subtleties and took on more of the character of naked combat of interests.

Perhaps the most independent but isolated slaves were the artisans. More than anyone else they were allowed to do their work on their own without supervision. Thus, in a sense they came closer to freedom but were less familiar with and found it harder to deal with manifestations of their bondage. Contacts with whites, if these went beyond the narrow patterns of every-day work, could produce tension or unpredictable behavior among the artisans. Table 2.17 serves as a rough summary of differences in attitudes by occupation. Since their jobs and re-wards were not the same, it is natural that house servants, skilled slaves, and field hands rated their masters differently. One should not read too much into this table; for Yule's Q shows a modest degree of association, and all former slaves tended to evaluate their masters in terms of the physical treatment they received. House servants and skilled slaves had a more favorable situation and thus tended to rate the master more favorably than did the field hand.

Supplementing the above information, a much larger body of material in the narratives demonstrates that class prejudices did not completely dominate the slave's psychology and that a sense of brotherhood with other slaves was widespread and sig-nificant. For many reasons class played a much smaller role than white southerners believed. Professor Genovese, in his study of slavery, accurately pointed out one of the major limitations on internal class divisions. Only on the large plantation could an extensive system of classes among the slaves exist, and such plantations accounted for no more than a minority of the slave population. Yet, for that minority Professor Genovese seemed to

Table 2.17 Occupation and Attitude toward Master (Yule's Q = 0.396)

| Occupation | Percentage | | Number |
	Favorable Attitude	Unfavorable Attitude	
House or skilled servant	73.6	26.4	891
Field hand	54.7	45.3	300
Total			1191

take class attitudes very seriously indeed. In his discussion of an aristocratic ethos absorbed by the slaves, he probably under-estimated both the amount of role playing that took place on plantations and the desire to satisfy white interviewers. Repeat-edly in the narratives the former slaves spoke of the concern for each other that united their group and ignored the supposed attractions of the big house.

Working close to the whites under their constant super-vision did not appeal to many of the slaves. It was easier to enjoy the fellowship of the black community in the fields and act as one wanted rather than as white propriety required. One former slave jumped at the chance to marry a field hand because, in her words, "I was tired livin' in de house where dey wasn't no fun." Field work offered some positive advantages over house duties: the field hands had a regular schedule and some free time to themselves, whereas the house servants always stood at the beck and call of the master. As one slave pointed out, the ambitious field hand could use his spare time "to earn spending money" if he wished, while the house servants "had no such opportunity." Another former slave, whose husband worked in the fields, was so determined to get away from house work and join her husband that she was "very rebellious toward her duties and constantly harassed the 'Missus'" until she gained permission to make the change.[29]

The narratives also make clear that on most plantations there was no sharp division between house work and field duties. Many slaves performed both tasks, switching from one to the other as circumstances required or even performing both on a regular basis. On a plantation in Texas, women always worked in the fields until their children had grown enough to take their places; then the women became house servants and worked at spinning and weaving. Many other plantations re-versed this cycle by putting girls to work in the master's house until they were "big 'nuff ter wuk out in de fields wid de others." Slaves who worked primarily in the house or the fields often had to take on the other duty for part of each day or at particular times of the year. It was common practice for masters to assign a certain amount of carding, spinning, or weaving to each female plowhand, and this work constituted her evening chores. The house servants, on the other hand, frequently found themselves in the field, particularly at cotton-picking time. "Mama was a field hand and a cook," reported one former slave. Another said, "I worked in de fiel' some, but mos'ly I was a house servant." Betty Guwn's interviewer discovered that this slave was "the personal attendant of the Mistress," worked in "a large Colonial Mansion," and had duties that were "many and responsible. However, when her house duties were caught up her mistress sent her immediately to the fields. Discipline was quite stern there and she was 'lined up' with the others on several occasions."[30]

In the shaping of the slaves' mentality there were cohesive forces more basic than the frequent mixing of house and field duties. An overall bond of empathy and fellow feeling united the slaves across class lines. For the great majority their common plight had generated a common outlook and a sense that blacks faced the same problems in relation to whites. Campbell Armstrong recalled that at the time of emancipation, "they all stood together. If this one was ill the others went over and sit up with him. If he needed something they'd carry it to him." It was notable that former slaves whose masters had treated them relatively well often went on to describe the abuses that took place on nearby plantations and the concern they felt for the slaves there. Despite the persistent efforts of their masters, the slaves stood together to a remarkable extent and refused to carry tales about each other. "In dem days ya kno'," said Reverend Ishrael Massie, "nigger didn't tell on each other." One of the former slaves interviewed by Fisk researchers noted that his master seemed determined to stop thefts and catch the culprits: "They give me a dime, quarter and anything to tell on them, but I told them I didn't see them stealing. I had though, and I would eat as much as any of them of anything they had stole." Another bondsman, who personally refused to help the others steal pigs, had no hesitation about telling a story to conceal the deed. [31]

House servants participated heavily in the process of spreading news among the slaves and concealing it from the master. From the house servants came some of the most vital information of all—advance warning of the master's intention to sell some of his chattels. After overhearing the master's plans, house servants often spread the word to those who would be affected. Susan Broaddus, a serving girl, once heard her owner spell the names of two slaves whom he was about to put on the auction block. Though she could not read, she memorized the letters and later slipped the news to her father. He understood and told the two men involved, who then ran away. This suggests the duplicity that many house servants regularly practiced. The faithful cook who defended her owners against critical outsiders was also likely to be a woman who whispered secretly with other slaves about freedom. [32]

Another manifestation of fellow feeling came in the efforts to help other slaves escape a beating. Task leaders, as Wash Ford testified, often took care not to get too far ahead of others working in the field. "If they didn't keep up they get a whoopin," Ford explained, so the "fast hand" who led the hoeing would "rest till they ketch up." Richard Mack stated that when he finished his own task, "I help others with their task so they wouldn't get whipped." There were some slaves who would not help the master catch or hold another bondsman who was to be whipped, and some individuals went farther. In Tennessee one slave grabbed a butcher knife and threatened the neighboring slaveowner, who frequently abused his slaves. On this occasion the woman with the butcher knife was lucky enough to get away with her impudence, and the slave on the next plantation escaped that beating. [33]

A frequently mentioned aspect of concern for other slaves

was the help given to runaways. On almost every plantation the slaves were quick to aid one of their number or a slave from another plantation who was in flight or hiding. Sometimes slaves stole food and hid it so that others who were underfed could "slip over at night" and get it. Runaways regularly enjoyed this hospitality. One man's mother, who was a cook, "was good to runaway slaves," and others told of feeding and harboring those who needed help. Clothing, food, and shelter were available to the slave fugitive from his fellows. Some, who dug caves in the woods, regularly obtained food from neighboring plantations and never had their hiding places revealed.[34]

The most striking proof of powerful group loyalty among the slaves came in an unexpected form. Repeatedly the former slaves engaged in bitter condemnations of some of their own people—the black drivers. These men had violated the canons of concern for their fellows, and as a result the former slaves almost wrote them out of the slave community. Not all of the drivers were disloyal to their people, but, according to the former slaves, those who became the master's man changed thoroughly. In so doing they earned the undying hatred of the other bondsmen.

Some black drivers, as the narratives show, attempted to juggle the demands of the master with the welfare of the slaves and find some way to help the other blacks. One account tells of a driver who faked the whippings he was supposed to give; another describes a driver who used to shoot cows at night and give the meat to the slaves. This man would "go 'round an' tell the slaves dey better go an' git some fish 'fore all go. Any time any one say e hab fish it wus understood e mean cowmeat." A third former slave reported that his black overseer saw to it that everyone had plenty to eat. But these instances virtually exhaust the favorable comments about black drivers.[35]

A far greater number of interviews with former slaves contain bitter remarks excoriating the drivers. "De overseer was a nigger and de meanest man, white or black, I ever see," said Jane Johnson. "Dat nigger would strut 'round wid a leather strap on his shoulder and would whip de other slaves unmerciful. . . . Dat nigger overseer was de devil settin cross-legged for de rest of us on de plantation all de time." Henry Cheatam painfully told of how a black overseer in Mississippi had made Cheatam's pregnant aunt lie down over a hole in the ground before he "beat her for a half hour straight till de baby come out raght dere in de hole." A woman named Mary Reynolds related that when she was young, other slaves in Louisiana warned her to be careful so that the black driver wouldn't "beat the breath out [of her] body," and a man named Simp Campbell expressed gratitude for a white overseer who restrained the driver's whipping. Other comments about the black drivers expressed similar feelings: He was "de meanest debil dat ever libbed on de Lawd's green yearth"; he was "the meanest of all"; he was "bad as he could be, an' de slaves got awful beatin's"; he was "a sorry nigger dat never had no quality in him a' tall"; and "we-all shore hated that old black man."[36]

The hatred of the drivers is all the more noticeable since the narratives contain scarcely one harsh word for the slave preachers. Like the drivers, black preachers were men in the middle. If they wanted to help the slaves, they also had to appease the master and carry out his wishes. Thus, slave preachers mouthed many words that the slaves dismissed as hogwash, but they did not dismiss the preachers. Knowing the constraints that affected them, slaves understood the preachers and appreciated services that they were able to perform in secret. Little of this kind of understanding seems to have applied for the drivers.

Of all the things that slaves hated about slavery, physical abuse came near the top of the list. The black driver was forced, by the circumstances of his position, to choose between inflicting cruelty on his fellows and giving up the various advantages of his position. The driver supervised *the* critical area of plantation life—agricultural production—and it is certain that the master watched his performance closely. If he wanted to remain a driver, he probably had to use the whip. This action promptly gained him the dislike of his fellows; thus, a spiral was set in motion that took the driver farther and farther away from the other slaves. Perhaps only those with a selfish and cruel streak could make the grade as drivers. One woman's grandfather quickly left the job because "he didn't wanter lose his religion trying to make slaves work." Those who stayed earned a long-lasting hatred. Sarah Ford told of the cruel driver from her plantation who had difficulty after the war finding any place to stay because "de black folks all hated him so dey wouldn't have no truck with him."[37]

Before ending this survey of conditions of life in slavery, a short comment on the relations between slaves and poor whites is necessary. Tradition asserts that enmity always divided these groups. The prevailing impression from the slave narratives, however, is that most slaves had very little contact with whites beyond the plantation and that the masters studiously tried to prevent such contacts. When these took place the slaves sometimes formed negative impressions, but certainly not always. In a surprising number of instances the former slaves told their interviewers of cooperative relations between the groups at the bottom of the South's social pyramid. To be sure, some narratives condemn overseers as "poor white trash," and the patrollers, who were well-established enemies to the slaves, often were poorer whites. But former slaves also tell of selling things to white farmers, thus making some welcome money, and occasionally working alongside them. "We worked and sang together and everybody seemed happy," said one slave. Another added, "De poor white folks was good to us, better'n rich folks. Dey'd give us a quarter now'n den." One man, a free black from Mississippi, even asserted that his family had sheltered and hidden Confederate deserters and draft dodgers. Perhaps Anthony Dawson put it best by saying, "Dey was all kinds of white folks . . . some of dem dat was poor would help you . . . but now and then they was a devil on earth."[38]

Anthony Dawson was rightly suspicious of all whites; for he knew that around white people, the slaves had to watch out for themselves and seize any opportunity to improve their situation. The plantation was the main theater of the slaves' lives, and there, through various means of resistance, they tried to alter their lot for the better.

3.

Improving the Conditions of Life:
Forms of Slave Resistance

North America's slaves did not passively accept treatment dictated by their masters. In the narratives, along with descriptions of the slaves' treatment and their feelings about it, there is a wealth of information testifying to a continual battle over the ground rules of plantation life. The slaves challenged some of the master's standards openly, struggled to subvert those that they could not overturn, and seized any opportunity that offered a means to improve their lives. In a thousand ways, ranging from subtle deception to bold defiance, they fought their owners. Many options, including successful revolution, were beyond the limits of possibility in the South; so the slaves used what tools they had in the arena closest at hand. Their resistance helped to shape the conditions of life on the plantation, and their wills often forced an improvement in those conditions.

Too often historians tend to define resistance by its extremes. The question, How did the slaves resist bondage? sometimes becomes, When did they stage violent revolutions? or worse, Why did they not revolt more often? To understand the slaves' resistance and assess its scope, one must accurately judge the possibilities open to them. Most former slaves interviewed for the narratives revealed that they had exhibited both a stubborn predisposition to resist and a sensible rejection of daring but hopeless action.

The slaves built a defiant mentality upon a sober appraisal of their situation. For example, one form of resistance which the former slaves often mentioned was running away; yet, the narratives make clear that for the great majority of slaves this course of action seemed totally impractical. "We knew we could run away, but what then?" asked a former slave. "[We] couldn't git away," explained another. Once caught, the runaway "was subjected to very harsh punishment." The odds did indeed weigh heavily against a slave fugitive. Held in ignorance, he had to travel great distances, usually at night, through rugged, unfamiliar territory guarded by patrollers and inhabited by the suspicious white majority. As one man said, the whites "had a 'greement" —both as a matter of law and custom—"to be on the watch for runaway niggers." They also had dogs that "would track you and all you got was a beating." Consequently, many slaves concluded that there was "no use tryin run off [because] they catch you an bring you back." Speaking for countless others, John White said, "I never tried it . . . I had whippings enough already."[1]

Probably a substantial portion of those who pondered flight reassessed the odds and chose, instead, to slip off and hide in the woods. The large number of reported instances of this behavior constitutes one of the important surprises of the narratives. Hiding in the woods represented a highly significant form of resistance. Part of this significance lay in the fact that it demonstrated the practical bent of the slaves. The bondsman who hid reversed the unfavorable odds confronting the runaway. Instead of journeying through strange territory, he could lurk about in his own neighborhood and use familiar paths and places of concealment. Rather than venturing out alone surrounded by enemies, he enjoyed the support of his fellow slaves, who could provide food, clothing, and information under cover of night. Masters, knowing that the odds were against them, frequently elected not to organize a search but simply waited for the slave to return or to indicate the conditions of his return. Compared to a flight for freedom, hiding in the woods was potentially less rewarding but definitely more practical, more effective, and more likely to succeed. In short, hiding was more appropriate to actual conditions.

The slaves designed their resistance to meet those conditions and combat the masters' actual advantages, which were formidable. The key to white control was its pervasiveness—the encompassing nature of the watchful white community. Everywhere the slave turned, a white man hemmed him in. "The white man was the slave's jail," said one former slave, who had identified an important truth. Of all the slaveholding portions of the Western Hemisphere, the American South by the nineteenth century was the largest in geographical extent and had the highest ratio of whites to blacks. The South also had a relatively small concentration of large slave holdings, which meant that from plantation to plantation a comparatively large number of whites came in contact with and watched over the slaves. The preponderance of power was overwhelmingly in white hands, so much so that some privileges could be allowed without danger. "Mos' ever plantation kep' a man busy huntin' . . . all de time," observed Charlie Davenport, but one individual's access to a firearm did not heighten the danger of mass revolt. The white population enjoyed the safety of numbers.[2]

Facts such as these defined the boundaries of reasonable resistance. Because radical redefinitions of their condition were impossible, the South's slaves had to wage a contest at the margins of their enslavement. They could not, in normal circumstances, destroy slavery; so they set out to weaken it. This decision should not be confused with the idea of accepting one's situation. The slaves did not accept their bondage, but external power left them few options. Knowing that they could not make themselves free, the vast majority of slaves struggled, instead, to lessen the extent of their enslavement.

Resistance, then, represented a wide variety of actions whose purpose was to improve the slave's lot. In differing ways, individual bondsmen fought to restrict abuses and improve their treatment. Many concentrated on limiting or ending the beatings so common to slavery. Others struggled to insulate some areas of life from the master's control and gain a measure of autonomy, or to undercut slavery and cheat the master out of the full value of his human property. Resistance covered a spectrum running from subtle forms of accommodation at one extreme, through secret collective opposition and overt confrontations with the master, to outright rebellion at the other extreme.

A broad definition of resistance coincides with the view taken by nineteenth-century southern slaveowners. To them the prime advantage of slave labor over free lay in the fact that slaves could be driven—"you could command them and *make* them do what was right." The slave by definition had no mind of his own; his will followed the master's will in all things, at least in theory. Free laborers could object and argue against orders, but the slave was required to be tractable, performing whatever the master directed. Commonly planters set minimum levels for work, such as three hundred pounds of cotton to be picked per day—a demanding task. Any labor assigned had to be performed or the slave paid the penalty. "Any slave . . . didn't done task," reported Gabe Lance, "they give 'em (with lash) . . . twenty-five to fifty. . . [and] less rations to boot!" To refuse to obey readily merited punishment; thus, the slaves' persistent and ubiquitous opposition constituted resistance in the true sense of the word.[3]

The varieties of slave resistance reflected the determination of people who were both stubborn and flexible, courageous and sly. The subtle and perceptive members of the slave community artfully developed skills of accommodation. This means of getting along with the master might seem a poor candidate for inclusion as resistance, but the slaves turned it to their advantage and used it to better their lot. Some built an advantageous relationship with the master by playing upon his likes and dislikes. The favored slave got away with many departures from plantation regulations because he knew how to charm or amuse the master. Others took care to present their case to the most

[74]

sympathetic white in authority, and skill in distinguishing marginal differences among whites seems to have been widespread. Playing the master off against the overseer, one woman in Mississippi, who had recently given birth, ran off after a whipping. When she came back, she went straight to her owner "and told him all about it," knowing that his concern for her and her child would seal the overseer's doom. In ten minutes the overseer was gone, leaving under a hail of curses. Another woman said, "Us most nigh allus tell de master" when the overseer became abusive, and some slaves even carried tales to whites who were not their owners. On Hagar Lewis's plantation the mistress regularly fed hungry blacks from other plantations, and the master prosecuted some of his neighbors for beating their slaves. Later during the war, the Yankees became a potentially sympathetic source to cultivate.[4]

Another subterranean but crucial area of resistance consisted in secret group activities of the slaves. According to some of the individuals interviewed, the interplantation slave grapevine did exist. "We used to carry news from one plantation to the other I reckon," said Phyllis Petite, "'cause mammy would tell about things going on some other plantation and I know she never been there." Cato Carter illumined some of the mechanics of this means of communication by explaining that, in his district of Alabama, slaves used "field calls and other kinds of whoops and hollers, what had a meanin' to 'em" to learn when it was safe to visit and share food.[5]

Special calls or codes also protected meetings among slaves on the same plantation. When blacks learned that their plans for a secret gathering had been discovered, the phrase "weevils in the wheat" spread this intelligence to the others. To protect meetings while they were in session, the slaves stationed on the path a "raid fox" or decoy—one slave, well-practiced in avoiding the patrollers, who would lead them off in the wrong direction. If the meeting was an important one, the slaves might use "niggers in relays from the trail to the meetin' place an' when the patrollers would show up, . . . the one farthest south would whistle like a bob-cat to warn the others."[6]

These meetings performed a very important function: they reinforced the mentality of resistance and strengthened the group identity of the slaves. Often the slaves met, not to plan some unique event, but simply to reaffirm the validity of their view of reality. Even those who felt they had a good master "want[ed] to git free and talk 'bout [things] in de quarters 'mongst [themselves]." By coming together in concealment, they helped make their secret lives and thoughts real, and thus gained strength to combat the master's propaganda. Often a white-controlled meeting occasioned a later, secret meeting whose purpose was, in effect, to set the record straight. White ministers, for example, generally hammered on the theme of obedience to one's master and mistress. After such services on Douglas Dorsey's plantation, "the driver's wife who could read and write a little would tell them that what the minister said 'was all lies.'" When a minister pressured slaves on William Adams's plantation into saying that they wanted the South to win the war, they quickly scheduled a countermeeting in the hollow to discuss their hopes for a northern victory. Other former slaves told of getting together in a cabin at night to sing, pray, and share their belief that "some day this yoke gwine be lifted offen our shoulders." In thousands of such meetings, "everybody talk 'bout freedom."[7]

Out of these gatherings came a solidarity that led to common activities aimed against slavery. One of the most widespread practices of resistance was theft, or what might better be called the appropriation or reappropriation of forbidden goods. Over one hundred former slaves spoke in the narratives about regular thievery, but this number probably underrepresents by a large amount the frequency with which theft took place. Reports of theft occurred proportionately more often when the interviewer was black than when he or she was white; therefore, many former slaves probably refrained from telling about an ordinary but much criticized event. Those who did tell about stealing agreed that it was common. Mrs. M. E. Abrams said, "We n'used to steal our hog ever sa'day night and take off to de gully whar us'd git him dressed and barbequed." Another former slave commented that it was "just natural for Negroes to steal."[8]

Plantation theft took place so often that blacks and whites alike knew a familiar song on the subject:

> Some folks say dat a nigger wont steal,
> I caught two in my corn field,
> One had a bushel,
> One had a peck,
> An' one had rosenears [roasting ears],
> Strung 'round his neck.
>
> Run nigger run,
> Patteroller ketch you,
> Run nigger run,
> Like you did de udder day.

Some former slaves had witnessed stealing so often that even as children they "would get together and laff about it," knowing that the joke was on the master and realizing that they must not breathe a word about late-night feasts. Because they recognized the ubiquity of theft and the difficulty of preventing it, some masters gave their slaves no more than "a little brushin'" when they caught the culprits. The former slaves described the pleasures of eating almost every kind of plantation produce—watermelons, eggs, chickens, sweet potatoes, hams, pigs, cattle, and corn. In addition, they admitted no guilt over taking "[what] they had worked for." "I don' think I done wrong," said Carter Jackson, "'cause the place was full of 'em [chickens]. We sho' earned what we et." To prevent detection, the slaves had evolved many strategies, from putting pepper in the dog's eyes to "clomp[ing]" the pig tight "by the snoot," in the words of Richard Carruthers, "so he won't squeal . . . while you knife him." Judging from the variety of these indications, appropriating goods was probably a common method of resistance.[9]

Similar gains in welfare for the slaves at the master's expense came from various forms of deception. The slaves had many ways of evading work and practiced them as relentlessly as the master labored to extend the work they did. One common stratagem was the shamming of sickness. Isaiah Green reported that his father, who was a valuable shoemaker, "beat ol' marster out 'o 'bout fifteen years work. When he didn't feel like workin' he would play like he wus sick an' ol' marster would git de doctor for him." This technique, which another slave said was used "often . . . to remain away from the field," probably worked best for the most valuable hands, whether skilled craftsmen or fertile women. As for the rest of his bondsmen, a master could simply refuse to allow rest or to call a doctor until the illness had become indisputable.[10]

A good deal of resting went on in the fields, however. Many slaves gained a brief respite by "lyin' in de corn row," but they had to remain alert for the return of the overseer. At cotton-picking time, those who felt overworked might avoid a whipping by sprinkling "the white sand of the fields on the dew soaked cotton and at the time it was weighed they were credited with more pounds than they had actually picked." Who can doubt that the careless, unintelligent labor by slaves, on which many travelers commented, was another way to lighten work's burden? Without much trouble the slaveowners could make their hands spend long hours at assigned tasks, but it was impossible to supervise each worker at all times and compel him to do his job skillfully. One planter admitted that slaves would "never do more than just enough to save themselves from being punished, and no amount of punishment [would] prevent their working carelessly and indifferently." By working below their peak efficiency, slaves were forcing a small improvement in the grueling, day-to-day pattern of labor.[11]

This kind of functional realism—a concentration on mundane but meaningful issues of plantation life—ran through the entire repertoire of resistance. It was the central theme of the slaves' relations with their masters. For the great majority of bondsmen, physical abuse stood out as the most galling and intolerable aspect of their exploitation. Again and again the former slaves evaluated owners in terms of whether they "whupped and slashed" or were prone to engage in other kinds of abuse. Accordingly, they directed most of their resistance toward stopping or limiting physical cruelty. Bitter arguments, tense contests of will, threats, physical violence—all served to deter whippings and beatings. Confronting their masters along an ascending scale of violence, the slaves directed their most vigorous resistance at the most oppressive slaveowners. As Beverly Jones put it, "Good masters had good slaves 'cause they treated 'em good," but "whar the ole master was mean an' ornery," his slaves proved also to be a troublesome and dangerous property.[12]

Though most resistance was directed against physical cruelty, a few slaves simply refused for personal reasons to take certain treatment and risked their lives in support of their determination. Many former slaves had heard of at least a few bondsmen who would not submit to the lash. The master stepped into unsafe territory or stood to lose valuable property if he tried to whip them. Other individuals sometimes reached a point at which they could not endure oppression any longer. Assailed by the patrollers, one young slave decided "dey was one time to die and he sta't to fight. He say he tired standin' so many beatin's, he jus can't stan' no mo." This man chose violent resistance but died as a result. Another former slave, Lewis Bonner, reported that his father, who had been whipped by the whites for laziness, suddenly broke and "just killed all of 'em he could."[13]

If harnessed and concentrated, such hatred could lead to revolt, but conditions in the South militated against it. The most notable insurrectionary incident described in the narratives focused, revealingly, on the alteration of plantation realities. A community of much abused slaves in Texas overturned the status quo on their own plantation. According to one of the slaves, William Moore, the master was "a terrible mean man" who "jus' 'bout had to beat somebody every day to satisfy his cravin'." After a mounting quarrel with the owner, Moore and his mother ran to the woods and hid for two or three months. Then the other bondsmen learned that the Civil War had begun and that whites were "fightin' over us niggers." Promptly they " 'clared to Marse Tom they ain't gwine be no more beatin's and we could come up and stay in our cabin and they'd see Marse Tom didn't do nothin'." Armed with shotguns, the two biggest men on the plantation forced the master to send away five whites whom he had hired to come and restore order. From that point on the slaves were in control: "Marse Tom cuss and rare, but the niggers jus' stay in the woods and fool 'way they time. They say it ain't no use to work for nothin' all them days." When emancipation came, all the slaves left.[14]

Aggregate data drawn from the narratives can supplement the suggestive information provided by incidents like the one above. The former slaves either spoke about resistance in which they themselves engaged or described the actions of other slaves on the plantation. As table 3.1 shows, the various reports provide a large body of data on slave resistance. This listing almost certainly is incomplete, for the former slaves discussed resistance more freely with black interviewers than with white; but it remains substantial enough to be helpful.

For a number of reasons table 3.1 should not be regarded as a precise count of the relative frequency of different types of resistance. One hundred sixty-six of the events listed involved resistance by former slaves themselves. Since most of the people interviewed had been quite young during bondage, their actions would not cover the full range of activity by adult slaves. Furthermore, conditions in the South changed radically from the 1850s to the 1860s. Successful flight became both more possible and more attractive; thus, the overall reports of runaways were pushed upward by the unusual wartime situation. To reduce these sources of bias, table 3.2 has been constructed to focus

Table 3.1   *Types of Resistance*

Types of Resistance	Percentage	Number
Ran away	41.2	340
Hid in woods	20.3	168
Stole	15.5	128
Struck master, stayed	8.4	69
Struck master, ran	1.0	8
Verbal confrontation	5.0	41
Fought patrollers or other whites	3.6	30
Killed overseer or other whites	2.4	20
Revolted or planned revolt	0.6	5
Committed suicide	0.8	7
Other	1.2	10
Total	100.0	826

more carefully on the actions of adults and on types of resistance likely to occur in normal times.

Still, this listing does not reproduce exactly the character of resistance on the plantation. The former slaves probably tended to recall the unusual but striking events instead of giving a careful and proportional account of every kind of resistance. Arguments with the overseer might have been weekly or daily occurrences; yet, less frequent occasions when someone ran away probably lodged more firmly in the mind. When former slaves like Adeline Marshall told of a suicide who "done hang himself to 'scape he mis'ry," they probably came closer to giving a complete and exhaustive account of that type of resistance than did those who spoke about stealing, which a variety of evidence suggests was very common.[15] Thus, the most frequent kinds of resistance are probably underrepresented, and one must use these tables sensibly and carefully.

What, then, can be learned from table 3.2? One salient fact

Table 3.2   Reported Resistance by Others

Types of Resistance	Percentage	Number
Ran away	28.3	117
Hid in woods	25.2	104
Stole	10.7	44
Struck master, stayed	12.3	51
Struck master, ran	1.5	6
Verbal confrontation	7.5	31
Fought patrollers or other whites	6.2	26
Killed overseer or other whites	4.1	17
Revolted or planned revolt	1.2	5
Committed suicide	1.7	7
Other	1.2	5
Total	100.0	413

Note: This list excludes those who ran away during the Civil War to join the United States Army.

is the close balance between running away and hiding in the woods. The frequency of reports of these types of resistance helps us gauge their significance. Although running away to seek freedom usually seemed futile to bondsmen, historians have correctly noted that it loomed large in the slaves' consciousness as a vital option, a course which always remained open if circumstances grew intolerable. Even those who never fled from the master knew well the tricks a fugitive should use. Rubbing pungent substances like turpentine, graveyard dirt, red pepper, or Indian turnip on one's feet was supposed to irritate the nose of the bloodhounds and throw them off the trail. "No bloodhound could trail a bit further after smelling it," Gus Smith confidently asserted, reciting well-established plantation lore.[16] Yet, hiding in the woods evidently held as important a place in the slave's mind, a fact which historians have not adequately recognized. In fact, running off to hide in the woods was probably more common than the table suggests, for the former slaves discussed it with more familiarity and probably omitted mention of many specific instances.

The practice of slipping off and hiding nearby played a key role in the slaves' struggle to improve conditions on the plantation. It was their most effective tool to goad the master into lessening his demands and loosening requirements. Some bondsmen simply ran off "to get a rest" from the burdens of work, but for most this act was far more purposeful. When a slave hid in the woods, he or she could count on ready support from the rest of the black community. As one informant described it, whenever slaves ran off, "next day Aunt Suke would be sho to go down to de spring to wash so she could leave some old clothes dar for 'em to git at night." Others testified that these slaves often came back "at night for to eat sumpin'."[17] Thus, the slave who hid in the woods had the capacity to maintain himself in reasonable comfort for an indefinite period and simultaneously deprive the master of his labor. While continuing to maintain the slave, at least partially, the master derived no benefit from his investment and expenses. This situation placed the bondsman in a strong bargaining position, and the narratives testify that the slaves used their advantage, regularly and successfully.

For the individual who encountered trouble, slipping off to the woods opened a way out and an escape from punishment. A foreman named Robert Scott, for example, jumped between his wife and the master to save her from a whipping. Enraged, this slaveowner ran to the house to get his gun; so Scott elected to "get out of the way for a day or two." Later, after passions cooled, the master realized that he needed his slave's skills, Scott returned without retribution, and his defense of his wife succeeded. Similarly, when a cook concealed herself in the canebrake for a couple of weeks, she escaped serious punishment on her return. Her master "was glad to get her back," just as most masters were. Frequently, the formalities of bargaining had even become explicit, for masters wanted their slaves at work and could not counter this kind of resistance. One man who ran off and hid several times described the routine: "Ah'd hide in the woods; then they'd send aftah me, and they say, 'Come on back —we won't whip you.' "[18]

Thus, the individual could bargain over the terms of his treatment. The technique of hiding in the woods afforded leverage against the master without serious inconvenience, and the narratives show that slaves clearly understood their advantage and exploited it effectively. On some plantations the bondsmen even managed to use this tool collectively to win benefits for the group rather than for a few individuals. "If we had an overseer that was bad," explained one informant, "the slaves would run away so's he'd have to get another one." By a form of strike these slaves served notice that their treatment was unsatisfactory and that "they wouldn't suffer it." The master relented.[19]

The ease and success of this means of fighting slavery led some to see further potential in it. One man whose master came to Texas when it was still frontier built up a close relationship with the Indians, put holes in his nose and ears, and occasionally "run off from his massa and stay with the Indians for weeks." Hiding had developed into an alternate form of life for him. Even without connections to another supportive culture like the Indians', some slaves chose to live in the woods semipermanently or permanently instead of existing in bondage. After digging a cave in a hillside, a South Carolina slave kept up contact with his friends and accumulated "a hog, two geese, some chickens and two middles of meat" before the whites caught him five months later. The whites never caught some of these woods dwellers, and several narratives tell of people who stayed in hiding until the war was over and then emerged "'thout no clothes on an' hair growin' all over [their] bod[ies]." Leah Garrett told of a man who established a real home for his wife in a cave complete with a stove that had a hidden flue: "He ceiled de house wid pine logs, made beds and tables out of pine poles, and dey lived in dis cave seven years [until freedom].

Durin' dis time, dey had three chillun." One former slave asserted that a man from his plantation lived fifteen years in hiding. Such a person might arm himself with "a scythe and a bulldog for protection," and the patrollers, despite their best efforts, could not catch him. The patrollers, as Walter Rimm explained, "wants him bad, 'cause it 'spire other slaves to run away if he stays a-loose."[20]

Not all bondsmen would choose this avenue, even if others had demonstrated that success was possible. Living in the woods meant a life of isolation and stealth. The fugitive gained freedom from slavery at the price of another kind of bondage, a life of many restrictions and unending fear of discovery. But the example of those few who left the plantation permanently served as a source of strength for those who stayed behind. It was possible to reject slavery entirely, even if most chose to endure bondage while fighting daily to change the routine on their plantation.

As table 3.2 suggests, the fight was often vigorous. Disagreements escalated at times into physical battles; slaves threatened and even struck their owners, which indicates how open the contest of wills became and how much ground the slaves had won for themselves. It is especially notable that the former slaves spoke more often of those who stayed after striking the master than those who ran. The slave who struck back did not suffer a paralysis of fear; it was not unthinkable to stand up to the master and fight. Mrs. Susan Hamilton recalled an eloquent cursing administered by one urban slave to her mistress. Outraged because her daughter, who had recently married, was sold away, this woman went into the street and shouted curses at "dat damn white, pale-faced bastard [that] sell my daughter who jus' married las' night." Beyond venting anger, such verbal confrontations could carry a threat. In Texas a field hand whose good work had kept him from whippings found one day that the mistress was approaching, determined to teach him that he was not immune to the lash. After arguing his case, the slave commenced "to wave he hoe in de air" and drove her from the corn-field. A venerable mammy on a Mississippi plantation reacted to a whipping by the young master by taking a pole out of the loom and beating him "nearly to death." As she flailed away she shouted, "I'm goin' to kill you. These black titties sucked you, and you come out here to beat me." Other narratives told of a female field hand who fought back during a whipping and beat the master into unconsciousness and of a man who choked the master to death for raping his wife.[21]

Violence commonly grew out of confrontations in the field over the amount and pace of work. Between the field hands and the overseer or master, a continual tugging and pulling took place. Some masters openly sanctioned this contest by requiring the overseer to establish his own dominance over the hands and never punishing a slave for hitting the overseer. Thus, when a new overseer took charge or when the regular overseer an-nounced new standards, the slaves quickly tested him and, if they intimidated him, won. In Georgia an overseer "attempted to whip one of the women but when she refused to allow [it] he never tried to whip any of the others." Isaam Morgan described another incident in these terms: a new overseer "tried to fight an' whip us slaves, an' one night six big nigger men jumped on him an' scairt him mos' to death."[22]

Life could prove dangerous for the master or overseer. During the war some slaves in Texas caught and killed "de old overseer [who] tried himself in meanness." Others met death in normal times as slaves turned their heavy hoes into dangerous weapons. The narratives tell of field hands who raised their hoes to protect the women from beatings or to fight back themselves. Some slaves knocked the overseer's brains out or "took an ax and cut off his hands and feet." Near New Orleans an overseer beat a woman "till the blood run off her on the ground. She fall at his feets like she passed out and he put up the whip and she trips him and gits the whip and whips him till he couldn't stand up. Then some the niggers throwed him off a cliff and broke his neck. . . . There warn't no more overseers on the place after that." On a Georgia plantation the slaves killed two overseers who had used the whip too freely. Thus resistance sometimes reached its extremes.[23]

Who engaged in the various forms of resistance? What were the characteristics of those who fought back? Tables 3.3 through 3.6 attempt to answer these questions on the basis of information supplied in the narratives. These tables show that the typical resister was an adult male who was married and worked in the fields. Though the young took action occasionally, parents and grown slaves shouldered the burden of opposing the master, and men assumed part of the women's share. In regard to the occupational background of resisters, table 3.6 demonstrates that no particular group held a monopoly on courage or pluck. Since field hands formed the majority of plantation workers, it is not surprising that they also represented the main source of opposition. But house servants and artisans were active in rough proportion to their numbers.

The primary purpose of overt resistance was to prevent physical cruelty or to strike back after it had taken place (see table 3.7). Verbal confrontations, fighting, and hiding in the woods—all might have this purpose. The runaways usually sought their freedom, and most theft had the object of bringing a better or more satisfying diet to the slaves. In addition, the slaves acted to protect members of their families, to stop sales, or to resist sexual advances by whites.

Slave women often enjoyed protection by their men, but, when successful resistance appeared possible, they were not backwards or hesitant in defending their own virtue. From the South Carolina narratives came a story about women defending their honor. The overseer, a "wicked man" who took "'vantage of all de slaves when he git half chance," followed two of the women who had been sent to pick blackberries, and demanded sex. "Finally he got down off'n his hoss and pull out his whip and low if dey didn't submit to him he gwine to beat dem half to

Table 3.3   Age of Reported Resisters (N = 413)

Age	Percentage
Child	0.3
Youth	8.0
Young adult under 25	3.5
Adult	80.6
Older adult	5.7
Young and old in group	1.9
Total	100.0

Table 3.4   Sex of Reported Resisters (N = 315)

Sex	Percentage
Male	58.7
Female	32.4
Both sexes in group	8.9
Total	100.0

Table 3.5   Marital Status of Reported Resisters (N = 193)

Marital Status	Percentage
Unmarried	13.0
Married	83.9
Both in a group	3.1
Total	100.0

Table 3.6   *Occupations of Reported Resisters (N = 127)*

Occupation	Percentage
House servant	22.8
Field hand	57.5
Artisan	18.9
Child's chores	0.8
Total	100.0

Table 3.7   *Purpose of Reported Resistance (N = 413)*

Purpose	Percentage
To avoid or protest whipping	55.9
To seek freedom	20.6
To supplement diet	9.0
To protect family	3.4
To avoid or protest sale	3.1
To repel sexual advances	1.9
Other	6.1
Total	100.0

death. . . . Finally dey act like dey gwine to indulge in wicked-
ness wid dat ole man. But when he tuck off his whip and some
other garments, my mammy and ole lady Lucy grab him by his
goatee and further down and hist him over in de middle of dem
blackberry bushes." Then the women ran to the mistress and offered evidence of their experience. Acting promptly even though
her husband was in town, the mistress fired the overseer and
sent him packing.[24]

As this incident implies, the differing roles of the sexes in resistance merit further attention. Table 3.8 specifies the male and female involvement in the major categories of resistance. Men, the evidence shows, proved more likely to participate in those areas of resistance that required strength and endurance; they predominated in running away, hiding in the woods, and joining in fatal confrontations with a white man. Women took more than a negligible part in these actions, however, and approached parity in the area of theft. In two categories—verbal confrontations and striking the master but not running away—the women predominated. Apparently, they were not afraid to argue their case or to strike out if provoked.

Table 3.9 presents the occupational background of the women who used force against the master. Since most of the women who dared to strike the master were field hands, not house servants, their boldness cannot be attributed to the liberties that grew from a personal, familiar relationship between the master and his house servants. Female slaves, with the assistance of their men, seem to have succeeded in winning some respect for their sex. Table 3.10 indicates that these women, like most field hands, meant their resistance to deter whippings or retaliate for prior physical abuse. They also, more frequently than the aggregate of resisters, acted from a purpose of defending either their virtue or a member of their family.

A final analysis addresses the question of what influence occupation had on resistance. The slave's work definitely affected his experience, defining the tone of his daily life and the quality of his relationship with the master. For field hands the continuing contest of wills over the plantation's routine was frequently open and harsh; for house servants it was generally more subtle and entangled in the nuances of personality. Artisans enjoyed the most freedom from supervision in their work and, thus, a degree of independence in their daily lives. Table 3.11 categorizes several kinds of resistance according to the slaves' occupations. Although the small number of cases permits only inferences

Table 3.8 *Sex of Reported Resisters—Selected Types of Resistance*

Type of Resistance	Percentage			Number
	Male	Female	Both Involved	
Ran away (including Civil War)	80.9	11.6	7.4	215
Ran away (excluding Civil War)	63.6	21.6	14.8	88
Hid in woods	69.6	24.3	6.1	115
Killed overseer or other white	61.1	27.8	11.1	18
Stole	53.3	26.7	20.0	30
Verbal confrontation	48.5	51.5	0.0	33
Struck master, stayed	35.3	62.7	2.0	51

*Table 3.9   Occupations of Female Slaves
Who Struck Master and Stayed (N = 19)*

Occupation	Percentage
House servant	31.6
Field hand	68.4

*Table 3.10   Purpose of Resistance by Female Slaves
Who Struck Master and Stayed (N = 31)*

Purpose of Resistance	Percentage
To avoid or protest whipping	74.2
To repel sexual advances	12.9
To protect family	6.5
To avoid or protest overwork	3.2
Other	3.2

rather than conclusions, some general patterns emerge from these data. Field hands exhibited the largest amount of resistance along the spectrum of opposition, while house servants took action as frequently, in rough terms, as their numbers on the plantation would predict. The behavior of artisans appeared more erratic, moving from one extreme to another. Relatively few engaged in verbal battles or challenged the master physically, but substantial numbers of artisans chose serious modes of resistance such as running away or becoming involved in violence directed at whites. Among the plantation's resisters, the artisans were most volatile, probably because their world embraced greater extremes of experience and therefore greater tensions. Compared to the rest of the slaves, they were "marginal

Table 3.11   Occupations of Reported Resisters—
Selected Types of Resistance (N = 175)

Type of Resistance	Percentage			
	House Servant	Field Hand	Artisan	Number
Verbal confrontation	13.3	80.0	6.7	15
Ran away (including Civil War)	17.0	47.2	35.8	53
Ran away (excluding Civil War)	25.0	39.3	35.7	28
Hid in woods	32.4	51.4	16.2	37
Struck master, stayed	25.0	71.4	3.6	28
Killed overseer or other white	0.0	78.6	21.4	14

men," permitted to taste more of autonomy yet held down indefinitely in slavery.

Thus, through various kinds of resistance the slaves endeavored to affect plantation discipline in their favor and increase the amount of living space for themselves. Concentrating on the restriction of physical abuse, bondsmen tried to compel the master to alter his methods of control. Evidence presented in chapter 2 indicates that they partially succeeded. Though most masters whipped at least occasionally, a majority of the former slaves rated their masters favorably in the matter of physical abuse. Although a few slaveowners depended heavily on the lash, most supplemented punishment with other techniques, such as surveillance and the encouragement of spying. Quite a few former slaves reported that their master had largely dispensed with whipping, relying instead on the threat of sale. "If Massa Jim had a hand he couldn't control, he sold him," said one woman. This threat, with its frightening implications for family ties, carried weight, but it also placed the master in a position that allowed him to act decisively only against major offenses.[25]

Slave resistance was both continual and shrewdly practical. In a variety of creative ways, the slaves developed tactics that could exploit what advantages they possessed. Concentrating on what was possible, the South's bondsmen kept up an unrelenting pressure that forced their masters to permit small but meaningful improvements in the conditions of life. Through such improvements they won significant ground in their contest with the master, ground on which they could build more firmly the foundations of a black community.

4.

Bases of a Black Culture

Southern plantations encompassed two worlds, one white and one black, one the master's and one the slaves'. At the core of the slaves' world was a strong sense of unity with the black community and a corresponding awareness of fundamental separation from white people. Even an orphaned slave girl who had been raised by her mistress instinctively left the whites when freedom came. "I knowed I ought to go to my own race of people," she explained. "I wanted to go to my color." Another former slave put the matter more forcefully: "White folks jes' naturally different from darkies. . . . We's different in color, in talk and in 'ligion and beliefs. We's different in every way and can never be spected to think or to live alike." Both these former slaves expressed their feeling that an essential difference existed between whites and blacks on the plantation and that their loyalty lay with members of their own community.[1]

This mental and social separation grew from and reinforced an underlying cultural difference. African culture had not been able to sustain itself in pure form under the unfavorable conditions of North America, but African descendants had built a black culture that could sustain their lives. Divided into hostile camps, blacks and whites developed separate systems of values and acted upon contrasting conceptions of ethics. Moreover, each group lived in a separate religious universe, although outwardly almost all southerners were Christians and Protestants. The slaves' culture involved different relations to the spiritual world, different attitudes toward nature and its powers, and a remembered connection with Africa. These and the conditions of daily life promoted the slaves' identification with the black community.

The power of the slaves' culture arose primarily from three sources: the fact of racial exploitation; surviving cultural differences between blacks and whites; and different religious beliefs and practices, whose influence carried over into daily life. These three sources gave the South's slaves in the mid-nineteenth century a sense of themselves as an independent entity and enabled them to build means to support their lives against the pressures of slavery. Moreover, through their sense of themselves as a people, the slaves found not only a source of strength, but also a set of common assumptions that would guide their actions for years to come. Black culture propagated the realization that white prejudice was entrenched and enduring, that blacks would have to move carefully in a hostile world, and that the white social system was designed to frustrate Afro-American destiny. As an oppressed racial group, blacks shared common ways of life and a common approach to society. They rejected white standards of conduct and avowed a black ethic that aimed at justice and functioned to sustain their community in its struggle against the white world.

More than from any other source, the slaves' identification with the black community arose from the kind of exploitation that they suffered. The whites defined them as a separate, inferior, and in many respects subhuman group, and this fact alone largely predicted the kind of response that blacks would make. Because white society shunted blacks off into a special and despised category, it was natural for blacks to see themselves as a group and to develop a critical perspective on white judgments. Southern slavery may have had its intimacies that flowed from daily association in close proximity, but it was rigid and unbending on the essential point. Blacks were slaves in the white man's eyes. Actually, all slaves were black, and custom and law decreed that even those blacks who were free ought to be treated as slaves. Compared to other slave societies in the Western Hemisphere, the South allowed far less opportunity for individual blacks to achieve desirable or varied status. American slavery was more than mere class exploitation; it was a caste system.

Eugene Genovese has argued that American slavery was a form of class exploitation, and by definition he was right.[2] But to leave the matter there is to miss the essence of slavery in the South. To be sure, class distinction has long been one of the most important sources of social division and conflict. It plays a crucial role in the formation of an individual's personality and point of view. Few forces can create the blind assurance that one's position is right or the callousness and indifference to others that grow naturally out of social class distinction. Yet, recognition of the power of class should not obscure the effects of racism, for racism produces divisions that are both deeply felt and relatively immutable. Men perceive racial differences immediately, often intensely, and it is a fact that men have great difficulty overcoming such differences. Modest variations in dress and deportment may identify the classes, but visible and permanent differences in appearance mark the races. In social terms it is possible for an individual to escape his class, but he can never escape his racial identity. Blacks bore their status plainly upon their faces for all to see, and the South had assigned a narrow and definite meaning to that status.

Southern society was organized first along racial, then along class, lines. Without exception whites dominated blacks, which is the essence of a caste system. Even among the whites, racism served as a fundamental support for the social system. Blacks knew that they were a despised race, oppressed for their skin color, and they dealt with the world on those terms, thus under-lining the gap between master and slave. Rejected by white society, blacks rejected white judgments in turn and developed their own moral system and mental world in opposition to the master's. The inclusiveness and power of American racism natu-rally stimulated blacks to draw together and build a life within their own group.

Whites directed racial hostility, not merely class condescension, at their slaves. Though a few of the wealthier and more aristocratic owners may have spoken caringly of their "black families," it was far more common for slaveowners to refer carelessly and contemptuously to their "niggers." On his travels in Tennessee, Frederick Law Olmsted encountered a woman who freely discussed her feelings while three of her slaves were standing in the room beside her. "I reckon that niggers are the meanest critters on earth; they are so mean and nasty," she said. "If they was to think themselves equal to we, I don't think white folks could abide it—they're such vile saucy things." Even the refined and genteel Mary Boykin Chesnut wrote that Negroes were "dirty, ugly, and repulsive" and "slatternly, idle, ill-smelling by nature." Viewing the black man as "a creature whose mind is as dark and unenlightened as his skin," Mrs. Chesnut concluded that "it takes these half-Africans but a moment to go back to their naked savage animal nature."[3]

The former slaves interviewed for the narratives had experienced many instances of this racial prejudice. They fully grasped the significance of degrading treatment such as that experienced by some who had had to drink milk from a trough, "a trough for de niggers and one for de hawgs." Others reported that their masters had lectured them on the theory that their skin color doomed them to perpetual bondage. As one man put it, the master "kept tellin' us a black nigger never would be free." With the approach of the Civil War quite a few masters evidently grew anxious over the status of their property, for the former slaves reported many outbursts. One man's master began to cuss and rave that "Gawd never did 'tend to free niggers." An angry mistress told Katie Darling, " 'You li'l black wench, you niggers ain't gwine be free. You's made to work for white folks.' "[4]

Naturally the slaves absorbed and reciprocated this racial hostility, and many of the former slaves discussed it, especially with black interviewers. Thomas Hall told his interviewer that "the white folks have been and are now and always will be against the Negro." In Tennessee one woman described her mistress in these terms: "Well, she was good as most any old white woman. She was the best white woman that ever broke bread, but you know, honey, that wasn't much, 'cause they all hated the po' niggir." Echoing these sentiments, a woman in Virginia remarked, "Course no white folks perfect." Anna Harris, still burning with resentment over the sale of her sister, said, "No white man ever been in my house. Don't 'low it. . . . I can't stand to see 'em." In a calmer vein Hannah McFarland of Oklahoma expressed the same attitude: "I can't say I lak white people even now, 'cause dey done so much agin us."[5]

Recalling their days in bondage, a number of the former slaves described the fear and reticence that they had felt around whites. Lizzie McCloud, who endured many whippings from her master, said that "white folks was the devil in slavery times. I was scared to death of 'em." For another woman this uneasiness carried over into Reconstruction when she went to a school for freedmen. "I wuz skairt [of the teacher]," she noted, "'cause he was a white man." The sense of foreboding around white people, the worry that ill would flow from encounters with whites, led many slaves to try to minimize such contacts. Some of the former slaves recalled that they had drawn back from closeness with whites to stay within their own group. As a young girl, Virginia Sims had refused to kiss the departing master and had blurted out, "I ain't goin' to kiss no white man." Another former slave deprecated the tendency of the master's sons to "want to mix in wid de 'fairs of slave 'musements," for he preferred to keep black and white socializing separate.[6]

In pulling back from unnecessary encounters with whites, the slaves cast their lot more completely with their own group. They knew that in the face of almost total animosity from the whites, they would have to rely on men and women of the same color to better their lives and find sympathetic hands and hearts. The degree of cohesion among the slaves was high (see chapter 2), and remarkably few bondsmen betrayed their brothers to gain small rewards from the master. "You see we never tole on each other," reported Jennie Patterson. Another woman named Jane Pyatt spoke poignantly of the way bondsmen treated each other: "The respect that the slaves had for their owners might have been from fear, but the real character of a slave was brought out by the respect they had for each other. Most of the time there was no force back of the respect the slaves had for each other, and yet, they were for the most part trustful, loving and respectful of each other."[7]

More striking evidence of the loyalty among blacks appears in the cooperation and mutual aid that existed between free blacks and slaves. Although slaves and free blacks rarely knew each other very well, due to the determined efforts of southern whites to prevent all contact, the two groups counted on each other for support and aided each other when possible. One woman who had struggled in poverty as a free black near Goldsboro, North Carolina, recalled that she liked to visit a neighboring plantation "'cause we was always hungry an' de slaves would give us somepin' to eat." In one part of Virginia after the war, the situation was reversed as a free black landowner, who had built up his acreage against great odds, voluntarily sold nearly two hundred acres to former slaves whom he barely knew. "I don't reckon he got all his money 'cause none of them had any," said the man's son. Nevertheless, this man extended his generosity knowing that "this was about the only land around here they could buy. . . . White folks wasn't lettin' Negroes have nothing." Thus out of racial exploitation the slaves created an important and beneficial bond.[8]

Yet, the connections within the black group also drew strength from underlying cultural ties that had been a vital part of the blacks' past and remained, on the eve of the Civil War, a meaningful element in their present. The narratives show plainly that African culture maintained its influence on the slaves. Just how much of the slaves' culture was purely African in origin is far more difficult to determine. After almost two and a half centuries of experience in America, the heritage of Africans, Indians, and Europeans had become thoroughly entangled. Many practices or beliefs that were essentially African had received an overlay of Indian or European culture or both. By the middle of the nineteenth century southern whites had borrowed large parts of African culture. Africans had learned from and intermarried with Indians, and all three groups had contributed some elements to a common culture. The slaves did not live totally within this common heritage, for many of their beliefs and activities, both mundane and ritual, were foreign to the whites and marked the slaves' African roots. But it is difficult to isolate many practices that were purely African in origin, since a melding of different peoples had long been underway.

Some of the purest elements of African culture manifested themselves in the areas of dress and recreation. For both men and women, Africans had distinctive ways of wearing their hair that neither Indians nor Europeans shared. Occasionally, men on the plantation would tie their hair up in a fashion similar to the cornrows of today. Not all the men adopted this style. Many saved time by not bothering with their hair, and one former slave suggested that only "some o' de old men had short plaits o' hair." Among the women, African styles of hair dressing were very common. "In dem days all de darky wimmens wore dey hair in string," said Gus Feaster. "In string" meant that the women tied small bunches of hair with string or small pieces of cloth. In addition, most of the women and some of the men wore head rags or head kerchiefs. Frederick Law Olmsted observed that male slaves in Virginia wore handkerchiefs on their heads "frequently, and the women nearly always." Along the lower Mississippi, he noted that these head cloths were wrapped in "turban-fashion," and surviving drawings of such headdresses show patterns of color and binding that are virtually identical to West African styles. [9]

In music and dance the African influence was also pronounced. Slaves had to make their own musical instruments from materials at hand; so naturally their designs followed African models that they had known. Stringed instruments similar to the banjo bore a close resemblance to the African "molo" or to African mandolins. At the end of the fingerboards of such instruments, slaves often carved figures or motifs that obviously were not of European inspiration. Southern bondsmen made drums out of hollowed tree trunks with a covering of stretched animal skin, and these drums plainly followed the design of African instruments. Gourd rattles also showed signs of the African influence.[10]

The dancing of slaves was so distinctive, striking, and unusual that it excited frequent comment by whites. Only the blacks were capable of the vigorous, athletic dances with complicated rhythms that set white observers wondering. Shaking their limbs in frenzied motion, the slaves carried forward a tradition in dance that was completely outside the European experience. One northerner who moved to Georgia in the late 1860s observed a patently African dance by blacks on his farm:

A ring of singers is formed . . . and they . . . walk slowly around and around in a circle. . . . They then utter a kind of melodious chant, which gradually increases in strength, and in noise, until it fairly shakes the house, and it can be heard for a long distance. This chant is responded to at intervals. . . . The dancers usually bend their bodies into an angle of about forty-five degrees, and thus bent, march around, accompanying their steps, every second or so, with a quick, jerking motion, or jump, which I can compare to nothing else than the brisk jumping of a frog. . . . The songs are mere repetitions of meaningless sentences . . . handed down by tradition from their ancestors.[11]

Former slaves often spoke in the narratives of their pleasure in dancing and of the way the owner and other whites marveled at the dancers' prowess.

In regard to attitudes about nature and the natural world, slaves also preserved a number of elements of African culture. Ghosts or apparitions were a part of reality more often for them than for white people, and some blacks believed that only they were able to see those spirits. "T'aint no use fer white folks to low dat it ain't no haints," argued Mrs. M. E. Abrams, because "de white folks doesn't have eyes fer sech as we darkies does."[12] More than two hundred former slaves spoke about "haunts," often at some length, and denials that ghosts and spirits existed came from a much smaller number. Probably the number of former slaves who described experiences with haunts would have been considerably larger than the total shown in table 4.1 had complete confidence and candor prevailed in each interview.

Spirits appeared in various forms; nevertheless, there was a substantial amount of consistency among the numerous reports. Jordan Smith, who had been a slave in Georgia, summed up the typical descriptions when he asserted that they sometimes looked "like a dog or cat or goat or like a man. . . . One time," he continued, "I looked and see a man walkin' without a head." Many other slaves sighted headless cows whose odd appearance and eerie silence were disturbing. The bodies of spirits could be either solid or vaporous and insubstantial. "Sometime dey looks nat'ral and sometime like de shadow," said Susan Smith, who added that a whitish, foggy shape might materialize if one looked steadily at it. Haunts appeared in two colors, either white or black, and if black their darkness cloaked them in a striking, impenetrable manner. A husband and wife described one ghost as "the blackest thing you ever saw."[13]

Table 4.1 Expressed Attitudes toward Haunts

Attitude	Number	Percentage
Believes in and sees haunts	134	51.9
Believes in haunts	68	26.4
Denies belief but knows others who do believe in haunts	9	3.5
Does not believe in haunts	47	18.2
Total	258	100.0

These apparitions also produced characteristic nonvisual effects such as noises, winds, and changes in temperature. "Dey makes de air feel warm," noted Susan Smith, and Prince Bee elaborated by saying, "Sometimes the noises would be right by my side and I would feel like a hot wind was passing around me, and lights would flash all over the room." The narratives refer at times to well-known individuals, such as the master, who came back after death, but frequently haunts were anonymous or, rather, had their own identity. They could become quite familiar to human beings, as Solbert Butler explained: "I see 'em all de time. Good company! I live over dere by myself, an' dey comes in my house all de time. . . . Dey play. Dey dance 'round an' 'round. Dey happy all right. But dey'll devil you, too. When dey find out dat you scary, dey'll devil you." To keep the spirits from being frightening, one had to stand up to them and put them in their place.[14]

In many of the narratives that dealt with haunts, there was a suggestive evocation of the religious belief in the living-dead that was widespread in western Africa. According to John S. Mbiti, author of *African Religions and Philosophy*, "The departed of up to five generations . . . are in the state of personal immortality, and their process of dying is not yet complete." These living-dead constitute a man's "closest links" to the spirit world and can still "speak the language of men" because they are still " 'people' and have not yet become 'things,' 'spirits' or 'its.' " As beings with "a foot in both worlds," they can visit mankind, but their appearance is "not received with great enthusiasm" and can become unpleasant. Several former slaves insisted that the haunts that they saw were the spirits of men formerly alive and now in the process of walking about on the earth before fulfilling their destiny. "Eve'ybuddy in de worl' hab got a sperit what follow 'em roun'," explained one man. Another former slave added that "de sperit uv de body travels en dat de truth." According to Caroline Holland, ghosts were "peoples dat can't quite git in heaben, an' dey hadda stroll 'roun' little longer on de outside repentin'."[15]

As the reference to repentance suggests, some discussions of spirits displayed the influence of the Christian religion. One woman combined African and Christian ideas in rather even-handed fashion when she explained that ghosts were "spirits in distress," and that a man who was "killed befo he is done what de good Lawd intended for him to do" would come back "to find who done him wrong." Several devout slaves who described their conversion experiences seemed to blend the concept of the living dead and the symbolism of baptism. They spoke of themselves as having "two bodies," but one of these was "dangling over hell and destruction" before God's grace allowed them to find the path to salvation. For these individuals the Christian notion of a burial of the old body in baptism and a rebirth in Christ had incorporated African ideas to the point that the one was inextricable from the other.[16]

Conjuration, however, revealed an unmistakable connection with Africa. Not all the slaves practiced or believed in conjuration, and the former slaves generally acknowledged that voodoo or hoodoo men were concentrated in areas of heavy importations or large black populations, such as the South Carolina coast and Louisiana. But for many slaves the conjure man possessed a power over nature that was unfamiliar to whites. Through the ritualized use of certain substances and the casting of spells or repetition of incantations a person could gain protection from harm, obtain the favor of friends, or inflict illness on enemies. The power of a *hand* (a bag containing items relating to the object of the conjuration) or a spell was awesome to those who believed.

The conjure man did his work aided by combinations of ordinary and unusual substances. "Dey uses hair and fingernails and tacks and dry insects and worms and bat wings and sech," said William Easter. Emmaline Heard's father once witnessed another slave mixing a powder composed of dried grasshoppers, spiders, scorpions, and snake heads. The prescription for a powerful hand or *jack* ran as follows: "Git snakeroot and sassafras and a li'l lodestone and brimstone and asafoetida and resin and bluestone and gum arabic and a pod or two red pepper. Put dis in de red flannel bag, at midnight on de dark of de moon, and it sho do de work." Another former slave described gatherings of "de old folks" at which the conjurer tied a black cat into a sack and threw it into "a pot of boiling hot water alive." After the meat had been cooked from the bones "dey took one of his bones . . . and put it 'crossways in their front teeth while dey mumbled sometin' under their breath." Then the bone possessed great power as a charm against the master.[17]

With such implements of magic the conjurers could produce powerful effects on their enemies. Rosanna Frazier believed that an "old, old slewfooted" conjure man from Louisiana robbed her of her sight by passing powdered rattlesnake dust through her hair. A slave from Louisiana testified that the old conjurers were able to make "you dry up and die 'fore you time. Dey take your strengt'. Make you walk on hands and knees." If so inclined the conjurers could give pneumonia, boils, or bad luck or put maggots or snakes into someone's body. A former slave in Georgia told of her sister who became ill and grew steadily worse despite the efforts of several doctors. At her sister's bedside this woman saw "small spiders crawlin' out of her mouth and nose. . . . That happened on Thursday and that Friday when she died a small snake came out of her forehead and stood straight up and stuck his tongue out." A conjurer from South Carolina had caused her death.[18]

Not all the conjurers' tricks had such sinister intent. Some slaves made up hands to help them please the mistress, and the conjurers sometimes sold jugs of "hush water," which the men would buy to give to their wives to make them "quiet an' patient." Wearing snakeskins supposedly prevented the voodoo doctor from casting his spell, and a bag of devil's snuff and cotton stalks hidden under the front steps could "make all who came up the steps friendly and peaceable even if they should happen to be coming on some other mission."[19]

On some plantations conjurers tried to work their magic on the master, with occasionally disastrous results. In one part of Texas "old black Tom" tied a string around a special bottle and watched the direction in which this jack twisted to learn whether certain slaves were going to suffer a whipping. On another Texas plantation a woman who had a hand designed to prevent whippings sassed the master because she felt safe. Immediately he whipped her, and "dat ruint de conjure man business." Similarly, the "Conjin 'Doc'" on a South Carolina plantation put a spell on the master to prevent his knowing that the slaves were stealing and barbecuing a pig every Saturday night. After a few weeks, however, the master began counting his pigs and then caught and whipped the culprits. Nevertheless, at least one former slave asserted that, even if the conjure men could not control the master, "they could make Negroes crawl to them."[20]

Belief in conjuration was probably rather common among the slaves. Long after emancipation a sizeable number of the former slaves who were interviewed discussed their belief in conjuring, and of those who dealt with the subject, a smaller number denied that such powers existed. A large number of former slaves also believed in signs, or events that predicted death and other important happenings. Table 4.2 summarizes these attitudes.

Some of the former slaves explicitly suggested that conjuring originated in Africa. A number of informants agreed that the older slaves were most thoroughly versed in this magic, and Rias Body explained that the old doctors had brought their knowledge directly from Africa or absorbed it from African forebears. It is also likely, as another informant asserted, that slaves imported from the West Indies, where the heavy concentration of Africans had favored cultural preservation, brought many of the hoodoo or voodoo practices into the United States.[21]

Table 4.2   *Expressed Attitudes toward Conjuring,*
Signs, and Superstitions

Attitude	Number	Percentage
Believes in conjuring	89	28.7
Does not believe in conjuring	61	19.7
Believes in signs and superstitions	137	44.1
Admits others believe in signs and superstitions	23	7.4
Total	310	99.9

Another practice common among the slaves exhibited a greater degree of mixing of cultural influences. Three hundred sixteen of the narratives gave prescriptions for various root medicines, teas, or tonics. A sizeable proportion of these prescriptions probably represented African lore transmitted and adapted to the southern United States, but many others were the common property of Indians and Europeans. Struggling against disease in an era of primitive scientific medicine, white settlers may have been receptive to any cure that seemed to work, and the therapeutic properties of certain herbs had been well known in Europe. Whatever the explanation, by the mid-nineteenth century southern whites themselves had developed a large number of recipes for tonics and teas. Often the slaveowners prescribed certain remedies for their bondsmen; yet, some narratives report that the slaves carried on their own medical activities apart from the masters.

Solomon Caldwell of South Carolina offered a typical description of the slaves' use of roots, herbs, and plants: "I 'member my ma would take fever grass and boil it to tea and have us drink it to keep de fever away. She used branch elder twigs and dogwood berries for chills." Additional remedies were legion and included tea made from rue for stomach worms, corn-shuck tea for measles, fodder tea for asthma, goldenrod tea for chills and fever, richet-weed tea for constipation, comfrey poultices for boils, garlic tea for worms and pneumonia, boneset tea for colds, blacksnake root for childbed fever, calamus root for indigestion, and many others. Although some of the recipes seemed unpromising or bizarre, the former slaves generally placed great faith in their effectiveness. [22]

Several types of evidence support the idea that at least some of these root medicines had originated in African practices and lore. Testifying to family traditions that had been handed down to her, one woman asserted that her mother had gained her knowledge from "old folks from Africy" and from the Indians. Many narratives agree that the oldest slaves on the plantations had the greatest skill in root doctoring and if this art derived from African cultures, its strongest manifestations would have been among the early generations. A connection with conjuration was also probable, for roots and other substances boiled together could be used to cast a spell. Repeatedly, the former slaves mentioned blacksnake root or Sampson snake root as primary ingredients, and the snake, as a symbol of the umbilical cord and the rainbow, held great significance in Africa. Perhaps also the metal, such as a string of coppers or a silver coin, that many slaves wore around their necks to ward off illness derived from the decorative customs of certain African tribes. [23]

The culture of Africa lingered among the slaves and affected them in ways both direct and indirect. Without a conscious realization of their African component, some slaves continued practices that indicated transatlantic values, such as carrying snakes or turning a pot down outside the door to ensure secrecy. Sixty-six of sixty-nine former slaves who mentioned this last device claimed that its purpose was to muffle sounds, but clearly a small pot could not contain the noise of several people singing or shouting in a small room. The use of pots in many West African religious ceremonies was probably a more reasonable explanation of the American practice. At a more conscious level, the slaves showed the respect for parents and grandparents that was typical of African culture, and some families tolerated considerable inconvenience in order to care for their elders and keep the family together.[24]

Finally, a number of former slaves wondered openly about Africa and felt a lingering fascination about the land of their ancestors. Those whose parents or grandparents had been born in Africa usually spoke of the fact, especially if there was royalty in the family's line. Amie Lumpkin, a slave in South Carolina, told of a bondsman who ran away from Charleston and headed North, intent on earning enough money to sail back to Africa. Years later, after emancipation, a few of the former slaves or their children did manage to visit the land of their origin and displayed considerable interest in it.[25]

Thus, surviving elements of African culture exerted a steady influence on the slaves (and their descendants) and helped to give them a sense of themselves as a separate group. Did the slaves feel that they were Africans and part of a living culture on a foreign shore? They probably did not, for the influence of African culture had become too fragmentary and disjointed by the middle of the nineteenth century to stand entirely on its own. But America's slaves knew that they were different in various ways from the whites. This knowledge, added to the sense of identity generated by racial oppression, bolstered their efforts to build a sustaining black culture.

The centerpiece of this black culture that the slaves developed was religion. More than anything else religion was the guide for their lives as a people, and it provided the cement that held them together in the face of disasters. It is difficult for secular twentieth-century observers to imagine how thoroughly religion permeated the lives of many of the slaves or how comprehensive its role was for them. Yet, the narratives offer abundant evidence that religious faith was the primary concern for many individuals and that it provided the group with a vision of right and wrong that broke through the slaveowner's efforts at control. Armed with their religion, the slaves established a set of ethics and a view of the universe that gave them spiritual independence from white propaganda and oppression.

In the narratives hundreds of former slaves testified that they had made religious activity a nearly constant part of their lives. Andrew Moss, who was in bondage in Georgia, described slaves who would "pray in de field or by de side of de road" in the midst of their duties. Others had "prayer grounds," he said. "My Mammy's was a ole twisted thick-rooted muscadine bush. She'd go in dar and pray for deliverance of de slaves. Some colored folks cleaned out knee-spots in de cane breaks," and in Louisiana slaves used "big holes in the fields they gits down in and prays." Clayborn Gantling asserted that he heard slaves praying "morning and night. Some of 'em would stand up in de fields or bend over cotton and corn and pray out loud for God to help 'em." Frightened of the overseer, field hands would "fall down on one knee and pray" in the morning on the way to the fields or wait "until the overseer got behind a hill" and then "lay down our hoe and call on God to free us." Many of those who had been children in slavery recalled waking up at night and hearing their parents in prayer.[26]

These impassioned prayers generally had to be offered in secret, since the master might punish any activity that could be connected with the desire for freedom. To escape detection some bondsmen actually put their heads into pots before praying or turned the wash pot "down to the ground to cotch the voice." After humming " 'ligious songs low like when workin'," the slaves later slipped off to secret prayer meetings, and the singing of "Steal Away to Jesus" signified that "dere gwine be a 'ligious meetin' dat night." "In de woods" or "way down in de swamps" the slaves could "sing and pray to our own liking." On through the night the bondsmen prayed, waiting to feel God's spirit and gain His support, as this song reveals:

My sister, I feels 'im, my sister, I feels 'im;
All night long I've been feeling 'im;

Jest befoe day, I feels 'im, jest befoe day I feels 'im;
The Sperit, I feels 'im, the sperit I feels 'im![27]

The subject of most of these prayers was freedom, the heartfelt yearning of the slaves to escape their bondage. Despite all their suffering the slaves somehow maintained a faith that God would deliver them. "I thought it was foolishness then," admitted one informant, "but the old time folks always felt they was to be free. It must have been something 'vealed unto 'em." After praying long and hard, Fannie Moore's mother suddenly saw a vision while she was working in the fields, and the Lord told her that she would be free. She told this to the master, who beat her, but she made no sound and "jes go back to de field a singin'" and exulting. "I's saved. De Lawd done tell me I's saved." After emancipation many solemnly agreed with George Strickland that "hit was de plans of God to free us niggers an' not Abraham Lincoln's."[28]

This religion that nourished the slaves held out a vision of a divine order very different from the white man's world. God's kingdom was independent of man's, and the slave worshiped in a religion of justice instead of the slaveowners' religion, which justified oppression. Laughing at the absurdity of white beliefs, one man observed in disbelief that "de white folks what owned slaves thought that when dey go to Heaven de colored folks would be dar to wait on 'em." Obviously, God's law would not sanction the injustice that took place on man's earth.[29]

Accordingly, the idea of retribution played a healthy role in the slaves' religion and allowed them to express the rage that they felt over mistreatment. A woman who had been sold from her family at age thirteen believed that the speculators who purchased her were "brilin in hell fur dey sin." "God's gwine 'rod dem wicket marsters," said another woman, and a man added, "God is punishin' some of dem ol' suckers an' their chillun right now fer de way dey use to treat us poor colored folks." Recalling the cruelty of his master, a slave from North Carolina affirmed,

"Well, I reckon he's found out something about slave driving by now." For those who broke God's law, on judgment day it would be "too late, sinner, too late, the train's done gone."[30]

Black religion also differed from white religion in its emotional content. For the slaves religious services provided a necessary emotional release to counterbalance the tense frustrations of slavery. They worshiped with their hearts, not just with their heads. One slave, whose master tried to tempt him into a decorous silence through the promise of a splendid pair of boots, determined to win this prize. But "about de middle of services, de old nigger couldn't stand it no longer. He jumped up and hollered: 'Boots or no boots, I gwine to shout today.'" Like him, other slaves took their troubles to secret prayer meetings and ended up becoming "so joyous," according to Richard Carruthers, that "they starts to holler loud and we has to stop up they mouth. I see niggers git so full of the Lawd and so happy they drops unconscious." Overseers sometimes caught the slaves during secret meetings when the noise became too loud, but the bondsmen had difficulty restraining themselves because their songs came "a-gushin' up from the heart." A slave from Texas reported that blacks in her area included an African-style dance as part of their services: "Dey gits in de ring dance. It am jes' a kind of shuffle, den it git faster and faster and dey gits warmed up and moans and shouts and claps and dances. Some gits 'xhausted and drops out and de ring gits closer. Sometimes dey sings and shouts all night." A few former slaves felt that religion entailed some Calvinist inhibitions, such as not playing the fiddle or refraining from dancing, but on the whole black religions thrived on a rich emotionalism that whites would not have tolerated.[31]

For their part, however, the slaves rejected white religion. They knew at first hand how much effect it had had on people who owned them, and they recognized the propaganda that whites directed at them. Almost all the former slaves were openly scornful of white religion as they had experienced it.

This scorn for white worship was one of the most consistent and vehement themes in the narratives. "You ought to heared that preachin'," exclaimed Wes Brady. "Obey your massa and missy, don't steal chickens and eggs and meat, but nary a word 'bout havin' a soul to save." Another man contemptuously said, "Church was what they called it but all that preacher talked about was for us slaves to obey our masters and not to lie and steal. Nothing about Jesus was ever said." Understandably, Tom Hawkins asked, "How could anybody be converted on dat kind of preachin'?" As the bondsmen recognized, the white man's message did not aim to spread the gospel but to make good slaves. God's truth was not available at white services, which explains Anthony Dawson's comment: "Mostly we had white preachers, but when we had a black preacher that was Heaven."[32]

Thus white preachers did not reach the slaves. When a northerner moved to Georgia after the Civil War, he found that the freedmen were hostile to his proposal of group Bible readings because they expected him to return again to the passages justifying slavery. The masters had abused the Bible so often that many slaves viewed the scriptures as a "slavery book," at least when it was in white hands. The white preacher's favorite message on theft also fell on deaf ears, " 'cause de stealin' kept goin' right on evvy night."[33]

This comment points to another important aspect of black religion. The slaves had developed a separate ethic in regard to theft, an ethic grounded in their resistance to oppression and their vision of a just world ordered by God. Because they had a religion that justified resistance and insisted on equity among men, they were not imprisoned by the masters' self-serving definitions of moral behavior. In the black community's estimation, individuals were not stealing from the master; for "all of it was theirn; they raised it." The slaves were "merely taking that which they had worked for" but which the owner unjustly denied them. "I don't think I done wrong," said Carter Jackson, and many others in the narratives agreed with him. Hunger had also made stealing food a necessity for some.[34]

Such attitudes were not the uneasy rationalizations of men who knew in their hearts that they had transgressed. The former slaves betrayed no traces of guilt as they discussed their actions, for they were part of a mental world removed from the master's and functioning on its own principles. An ethic of justice guided them, as opposed to the master's system of right and wrong; this ethic permitted "theft" but imposed its own constraints. The former slaves believed it was right to take what was theirs; they plainly did not feel that it was right to turn the tables and inflict great harm on the master, thus causing injustice to flow in the opposite direction. In the last years of the Civil War and the first years of Reconstruction, the vast majority of slaves followed their moral lights and did not take advantage of the planters' weakness. The slaves did not try to bankrupt their former owners or expropriate their homes and private property. They merely sought fair wages or hoped for a small piece of land that could give them a start.

In such ways the slaves' religion gave autonomy to a mental universe independent of the masters' and supportive of liberation. It offered solace for their grief but much more besides. It defined an ethical system that stimulated their resistance, and it provided a spiritual vision that affirmed the humanity and dignity of people who were struggling under a suffocating burden of degradation. The slaves' religion helped them to see themselves in a context removed from the slaveowners' crippling perspective, thus sustaining mental resistance when physical opposition was not always possible.

The black preachers played a major role in nourishing and extending this religious vision among the slaves. Trying to prevent just such an occurrence, the whites supervised black preachers closely and instructed them in what to say. But the audience knew that the speaker's heart was not behind the familiar words about obeying master and mistress, and the black preachers found means to bring a true message to their fellows. Through secret services and by taking advantage of other opportunities that offered themselves, the black preachers were able to escape the master's restrictions on their role. Virtually without exception, the narratives show a respect for the slave preachers, an appreciation of the difficulties under which they worked, and an understanding of their true role.[35]

When whites placed a slave in the pulpit after the white minister had spoken, "none of the slaves believed in the sermons but they pretended to do so." The listeners knew that "the white preacher would tell [the black speaker] what [he] had to do"; therefore, "if [slaves] had prayer meeting [they] would have it on the sly." Anderson Edwards, who was a black preacher during slavery, explained his role in this way: "When I starts preachin' I couldn't read or write and had to preach what massa told me and he say tell them niggers iffen they obeys the massa they goes to Heaven but I knowed there's something better for them, but daren't tell them 'cept on the sly. That I done lots. I tells 'em iffen they kepps prayin' the Lord will set 'em free." Apparently the preachers seized other opportunities to fulfill their true role, such as sitting up with the body of one who had died and talking with the deceased's relatives. Masters tried to restrict this visiting, "but urthur slaves would slip in atter dark." Through such means the minister was able to communicate with a large number.[36]

Thus, the black preachers augmented the effectiveness of the slaves' religion and helped it serve their needs. The ministers were a force that strengthened the slave community and worked for its liberation. As they preached to different groups of slaves, they spread the promise of God's justice and news of important events besides. "It was from this minister," noted Amanda Mc-Cray, that slaves on her plantation "first heard of the Civil War. He held whispered prayers for the success of the Union soldiers."[37] As so many of "the old time folks" had believed, the Civil War fulfilled God's promise and brought emancipation. During the war and the first days of freedom, the slaves drew on their separate culture and the fundamental things they had learned about whites to guide their steps. The next chapter treats the attitudes and actions of the slaves as they began carefully to find their way into an uncertain future.

Reproduced from the collection of the Library of Congress

"Seeing How the Land Lay" in Freedom

The Civil War and Reconstruction were signal events in the lives of the former slaves who were interviewed for the narratives. They had much to say about these crucial periods, and their recollections were often fresh and strong. They fully realized that the events of these years both altered the course of their lives, freeing them from bondage, and set severe restraints on their future, dooming them to a state of quasi slavery that fell far short of equality. In the stories they told as well as in traditional sources lie many clues to the frame of mind of the men and women who started this journey from slavery toward freedom.

Few white Americans, whether northerners or southerners, have understood the slaves' frame of mind during these critical periods. As outsiders, proud of their own good intentions and forgetful of their own faults, many northerners of the Civil War era simply assumed that the slaves would welcome them as liberators and boldly seize the opportunity to take a stand and live as free men. The books and diaries written by disillusioned northern do-gooders show that these expectations were not always fulfilled. Southerners, sure of their knowledge as insiders and dependent on a protective mythology about faithful bondsmen, generally felt certain that the slaves would remain loyal to their masters, the whites who truly cared for them. The disappointment of these expectations was often profound and baffling for white southerners. Later generations have gained little enlightenment, for the influence of the Civil War ran so deep that northerners and southerners tended to adopt the traditional outlook of their section of the country.

The slaves were not white men, reacting straightforwardly to unequivocal opportunities, as the northerners seemed to assume. Nor were they degraded and dependent retainers, full of gratitude toward their owners as some southerners believed. The slaves were an oppressed group with a separate identity, intensely aware of their status as a despised race, guided by their black culture, and conditioned by their experience to regard all whites with suspicion. The slaves broke with their masters because they were determined to end their bondage and win greater independence, autonomy, and opportunity for themselves. But they did not always act as the northerners had expected because they maintained a deeply ingrained suspicion of white people and a keen awareness of the persistence of old centers of power. Following their own lights, the slaves struggled to improve their position in a hostile world. Their approach revealed a penetrating assessment of the people with whom they had to deal and a shrewd caution. The freedmen looked about before taking action and assessed their situation with care in order to maximize whatever advantages existed.

After the Civil War broke out, southern slaves endeavored to learn all they could about the conflict that would profoundly alter their lives. A few may have obtained a sophisticated understanding of events; one narrative refers to Lincoln's colonization proposals, and the official records of the Union armies preserve the comments of Reverend Garrison Frazier, a free black minister from Savannah. Frazier met with General William T. Sherman and Secretary of War Edwin Stanton in January 1865 and precisely summarized the purpose of the war in these words: "The object of the war was not, at first, to give the slaves their freedom, but the sole object of the war was, at first, to bring the rebellious States back into the Union. . . . Afterward, knowing the value that was set on the slaves by the rebels, the President thought that his proclamation would stimulate them to lay down their arms, . . . and their not doing so has now made the freedom of the slaves a part of the war." Most slaves probably did not have this detailed understanding, but they knew that slavery was an issue in the war and that their freedom was at stake.[1]

"We children heard the old folks talking about it [the war]," said one woman, and another recalled "the whisperings among the slaves—their talking of the possibility of freedom." With thousands of southern whites enrolling, drilling, and marching off to battle, it was impossible to keep many facts of the war a secret. Bondsmen could also gain information by listening in on the whites "when they was reading their papers and talking after supper," and then the better informed slaves could spread the news. In Georgia one woman who had learned to read would steal the newspapers and inform her fellows of the war's progress. Knowing clearly whose side they were on, some slaves refused to pray for the Confederates, while others reported singing the pro-Union song, "'Gonna hang Jeff Davis to a sour apple tree.'" On Fanny Cannady's plantation one huge black man named Leonard commented bitterly on the master's son, who rode off to war in Confederate gray: "Look at dat God damn sojer. He fightin' to keep us niggahs from bein' free." Overhearing this remark, the master got a gun, "leveled it on Leonard an' tole him to pull his shirt open. Leonard opened his shirt and stood dare big as er black giant sneerin' at Ole Marse." Despite the mistress's pleas, the master pulled the trigger, and Leonard died "layin' on de groun' wid dat bloody hole in his ches' an' dat sneer on his black mouf."[2]

To hasten freedom, thousands of slaves decided to fight in the United States Army. This decision may not always have been simple or straightforward, for doubts about white people ran deep. Ambus Gray described hesitation on the part on slaves in his area, even after word got around that the North was fighting to give the black man freedom: "Some of em thought they said that so they'd follow and get in the lines, help out."[3] Nevertheless, from all parts of the South slave men decided to cast their lot with the Federals and ran away to take up arms. Some traveled for miles through Confederate territory while others came into Union lines nearby. In all almost two hundred thousand blacks, including many slaves, fought on the Union side and made an indispensable contribution to victory.

The majority of slaves stayed on the plantations and worked for freedom in their own way. Family responsibilities and the dangers of escape probably kept many from joining the Federals. Meanwhile, as careful studies by earlier historians have shown, plantation discipline deteriorated while southern slaveowners were away at war. As one former slave put it, "Us slaves worked den when we felt like it, which wasn't offen,"[4] and many white women had their hands full getting any work out of the slaves. In time the advancing armies reached a growing number of plantations, and the slaves came into contact with their liberators. This encounter was not always the joyous one that modern students might expect.

There is a widespread assumption that the slaves met the Yankees with open arms and launched into ecstatic celebrations and expressions of gratitude. Indeed, this sometimes happened, but such was not always the story. Though glad to be free, the slaves often hung back from their liberators and moved cautiously in the strange atmosphere. This reluctance to greet the Yankees sometimes confused masters and mistresses, who seemed eager to grasp at evidence of "loyalty" among their slaves. Years after the Civil War, Mrs. Irby Morgan proudly recounted the actions of her bondsman, Joe. Instead of rushing to meet the Union troops, he hung back and condemned those who ran forward for making "fools of themselves." "Now, if you please," he said to Mrs. Morgan, "look at the poor, white trash them niggers is running after. If they was in the gutters [the soldiers] wouldn't pick them up, unless they wanted them to fight for them. I tell you now they won't get dis nigger. And I thank God I know who my friends are." Joe doubted that the soldiers were his friends, and he had good reason to play up to his mistress; for he enjoyed an enviable position as errand boy and messenger, which often allowed him to be on his own and stay away from the plantation for periods of up to a few days. Yet, even to her he revealed quite clearly that his loyalty was based not on devotion but on the calculation that she would treat him better than the unpredictable soldiers.[5]

Similar suspicions led other slaves to move cautiously and watchfully around newly arrived Union forces. Southern propaganda had pictured the Yankees as brutal and barbarous men, even as monsters in semihuman form, but it is doubtful that any but the children credited such stories.[6] The slaves approached United States troops gingerly because they expected racial animosity from all whites and because the soldiers' arrival greatly complicated relations with the master. In fact, the actions of the troops often proved that the slaves' suspicions were well founded. In many cases an initial attitude of cautious observation had turned to active dislike by the time the men in blue uniforms left.

In state after state the former slaves told the same saddening story about their encounters with Union soldiers. When the Yankees arrived they brought theft, destruction, and even mistreatment of the slaves with them. Instead of acting as friends, the soldiers caused suffering and hardship for many bondsmen. In the context of the war between North and South, destruction of southern foodstuffs and property served to bring Union victory and emancipation nearer. But for the individual bondsman, Yankee depredations only made a burdensome life more trying still. How was one to eat after the soldiers had gone? In addition, there was considerable racism in the northern armies that found an outlet around the slaves. War had hardened the attitudes of soldiers who were tired, not always well-disciplined, and concerned most with their own welfare. To the slaves, the actions of United States troops were frequently appalling.

The "army . . . seemed more concerned 'bout stealin'," said one man, "than they was 'bout de Holy War for de liberation of de poor African slave people. They took off all de hosses, sheeps, cows, chickens, and geese, took de seine and de fishes they caught, corn in crib, meat in smoke-house, everything." Echoing his words one woman noted that after the Yankees left, "all us had to thank them for, was a hungry belly, and freedom"; another former slave observed that the soldiers "starved out more black faces than white at their stealing." With all the food and animals destroyed, slaves had to "scour de woods for hickory nuts, acorns, cane roots, and artichokes" unless their master had sufficient resources to buy food elsewhere. After taking "everything carryable off de plantation," the soldiers sometimes burned "de big house and de slave houses and ev'rything" in an orgy of destruction.[7]

One act that affected the slaves strongly was the mutilation of farm animals. Hungry for good, fresh meat, the troops naturally slaughtered some beef and pork, but the slaves were unprepared for the brutal way in which they did it. "I'se seed dem cut de hams off'n a live pig or ox an' go off leavin' de animal groanin'," remembered one man. "De massa had 'em kilt den, but it wuz awful." Similarly Adeline Jackson recalled that "de meanest thing I ever see was shoats they half killed, cut off de hams, and left de other parts quiverin' on de ground."[8]

The soldiers' thievery could and did affect the slaves personally. Poor as most bondsmen were, they had certain ordinary possessions such as shoes and blankets that were very attractive to a soldier on the march. John Bectom's mother kept a good pair of shoes in a chest, and a Yankee "came and took the shoes and wore them off, leaving his in their place." A young boy lost his treasured penknife, and Sam Word's mother saw her quilts stolen. This woman, irritated at one soldier's selfishness and lack of consideration, berated him with the words, "Why you nasty, stinkin' rascal. You say you come down her to fight for the niggers, and now you're stealin' from em." His reply may have stunned her, but it probably expressed the feelings of many of the Federals: "'You're a G—D—— liar, I'm fightin' for $14 a month and the Union.'"[9]

The slaves risked losing more than a few inexpensive possessions. Always needing additional manpower, the Union army viewed the slaves as a vital resource, and commanders impressed many bondsmen to carry supplies and perform fatigue duty. "If they wanted a colored man to go in camp with them and he didn't go," complained one former slave, "they would shoot you down like a dog." After burning the cotton and raiding the smokehouse, recalled another woman, "den dey pick out de stronges' er Marse Ned's slave mens en take 'em 'way wid 'em." Once in federal service, impressed slaves sometimes did not know what their fate would be. One group from Georgia accompanied the army as far as Virginia without ever knowing whether Sherman intended to keep them in slavery or not. General Sherman himself admitted that "it is hard to tell in what sense I am most appreciated by Sambo—in saving him from his master, or the new master that threatens him with a new species of slavery."[10]

As has been the case with invading armies throughout history, abuses of women also occurred. Bessie Lawson saw her mother whipped by federal soldiers and dragged off to their camp. Bessie's mother soon escaped, but not before she had been impregnated by her captors. Another woman's mother was carried off by the troops and never heard from again. Even when the Yankees did not mistreat slave women, they often frightened them by marching into the houses and searching the premises. To protect the women against possible rape or mistreatment, male slaves sometimes took precautions. On one plantation the black men gathered all the women together into one building and posted a guard.[11]

If the slaves did not cooperate fully and promptly, Union soldiers sometimes punished them ruthlessly. One black in Virginia gave false directions to Sheridan's men, "an' dey came back an' foun' him an' took a rope an' tied it to his two thumbs an' tied him up on a tree." This man "stayed there 'til he died. His fingers just dropped off." In Alabama, Federals suspended one woman by her thumbs because she refused to allow her children to be impressed, and another man suffered the same treatment because he would not tell where the master's money and silver were hidden. Racism motivated some of these incidents and often emerged in ugly ways. According to Mrs. Mildred Graves, "One time . . . five o' us colored girls was walkin' out, [and] some Yankees stopped us an' took razors an' cut us on our arms, legs, an' our backs."[12]

The accounts of these unpleasant encounters with Yankees came from every state, and as table 5.1 shows, more than 70 percent of the reported experiences with United States troops were negative. There was some tendency for white interviewers to obtain this information more often than black interviewers (for the former slaves knew that southern whites enjoyed hearing criticism of Yankees), but for each race the primary picture remained the same. After the slaves received such treatment from their liberators, it is likely that their deeply rooted reticence and caution around white people increased.

Of course, as table 5.1 also shows, the soldiers occasionally aided the slaves. Julia Woodbury remembered that federal offi-

Table 5.1   *Reported Experiences with United States Troops*

Experience	Percentage	Number
Theft	31.2	219
Destruction	7.6	53
Theft and destruction	18.0	126
Impressment of slaves	6.8	48
Other mistreatment	6.8	48
Caused no trouble	10.6	74
Told free	8.4	59
Gave aid	8.4	59
Took to camp for freedmen	2.1	15
Total	99.9	701

cers appeared in her section of South Carolina to divide corn and meat among the slaves. Others reported that the troops took them to freedmen's camps where they were cared for and had an opportunity to go to school. "Dey treated us all mighty good," said Tom W. Woods, who was on a government farm in Alabama. "We had plenty good food and clothes."[13]

But even when the soldiers tried to be kind to the slaves, they often placed them in a difficult position and exposed them to future reprisals. It was common practice for troops, on arrival at a plantation, to throw open the smokehouse and take the hams curing inside. Some sympathetic officers pressed food on the slaves and said, "'Why don't you poor darkeys take all de meat and molasses you want? You made it and it's yours much as anybody's!'" The slaves may have hungered for this food, "but we know dey [the soldiers] soon be gone, and den we get a whipping iffen we do." While the Yankees ate their fill, the master was waiting to come out of hiding. Similarly, when they questioned slaves about their treatment, the troops often ignored social realities. For example, when Lizzie Baker's mother was asked, "'Do dey treat you right?'" she answered "Yes," but only because "ole missus wus standin' dere, an' she wus 'fraid not to say yes."[14]

Though federal troops often offended the very people they liberated, there was much joy among the slaves over their release from bondage. Throughout the South thousands of blacks sang, danced, and rejoiced that their greatest hopes had come true. Martin Ruffin remembered the slaves on his plantation jumping and clapping their hands, and one man called out, "'We is free—no more whippings and beatings.'" For many, the end of physical abuse and slavery's other horrors deserved special thanks. On one Virginia plantation an elderly woman "who was near 'bout a hundred" summed up many reasons for rejoicing in words that became an impromptu song. The slaves were "all sittin' roun' restin' an' tryin' to think what freedom meant . . . [when] Sister Carrie . . . started to talkin':

Tain't no mo' sellin' today,
Tain't no mo' hirin' today,
Tain't no pullin' off shirts today,
Its stomp down freedom today.
Stomp it down."

The others then joined with her and made a chorus: "Stomp down freedom today / Stomp it down! / Stomp down freedom today." Singing late into the night, another group of freedmen invented this song:

Ain't no mo' blowin' dat fo' day horn,
Will sing, chillun, will sing,
Ain't no mo' crackin' dat whip over John,
Will sing, chillun, will sing. [15]

For others emancipation meant release from the irksome pretense of slavery, an end to laboring for a despised owner who could punish or sell a slave as he desired. One grandmother in Virginia, who was hired out away from home on the day she learned of freedom, "dropped her hoe an' run all de way to de Thacker's place—seben miles it was—and run to ole Missus an' looked at her real hard. Den she yelled, 'I'se free! Yes, I'se free! Ain't got to work fo' you no mo! You can't put me in yo' pocket now!' Gramma say Missus Thacker started boo-hooin' an' threw her apron over her face an' run in de house." [16] For both these women slavery's pretense was over, and the true feelings that had lain beneath the surface stood revealed. The slave no longer had to submit and mask her resentment for fear of being sold. Obviously her owner still felt the desire to control and dominate a human chattel, but she had lost the power and shrank from dealing with a disturbing new reality.

Yet, along with the joy there was another reaction among the slaves, an uncertainty that reflected their awareness of the dangers that lay in the uncharted course ahead. "When the war was over and the slaves called up and told they were free," explained Wheeler Gresham, "'sum wuz glad an' sum wuz sorry, dey all wuz at a wonder—at de row's en', didn't know whar ter go.'" Echoing these sentiments, other former slaves recalled that they had not been sure of "what to do," and Jane Johnson said, "I was kinda lonesome and sad lak. Us slaves was lost, didn't know what to do or where to go." Suddenly their whole world had changed, and no one knew immediately what the ground rules of the new era would be. Freedom at last had arrived, and blacks would have a potentially greater role in shaping their destiny, but the slaves knew in their hearts that some things would not change. Prejudice still ran deep among the whites, and only a dangerous process of experimentation and testing could identify the boundaries of this new freedom.[17]

Long and bitter experience had created an instinctual caution in the minds of the slaves. With shrewd appreciation of the obstacles that remained, they did not naively assume that freedom was total. Carefully, tentatively they would explore the limits of their freedom to act and grasp as many opportunities as they could find. W. L. Bost effectively captured the initial attitude of the freedmen: "After the war was over we was afraid to move. Jes' like tarpins or turtles after 'mancipation. Jes' stick our heads out to see how the land lay." Generations of enslavement had made it second nature for the slaves to assess the whites' attitudes, to study "how the land lay," and they did not discard this habit as soon as they were free. One former slave who was interviewed by the Fisk researchers explained that each slave was "wondering what he was going to do, for he still had to look to the white man." Much would depend, the freedmen knew, on their former masters.[18]

Even while the war was raging, some slaves had realized that in the future their lives and those of the southern whites would be inextricably linked. Martin Jackson reported that his father "kept pointing out that the War wasn't going to last forever, but that our forever was going to be spent living among the Southerners, after they got licked." These southerners, disappointed and embittered by defeat, would still hold tremendous power. They were the landowners, the educated and privileged group that was experienced in directing affairs. For years they had run society in their own way and then had gone to war to protect their control. Uneducated freedmen, who owned no property and had limited exposure to the world outside their plantation or country, sensed that the planters still enjoyed superior power. "'You got to say master?'" asked one slave in Georgia after freedom came. "'Naw,'" answered his fellows, but Sarah Patterson recalled that "they said it all the same. They said it for a long time."[19]

The Yankees had altered the balance of power by defeating the South in war and announcing their intention to supervise the reorganization of southern life during Reconstruction. But it was not at all certain that northern promises represented the new reality. Every powerful person whom the slaves had known before the war was a southerner. The individuals who most affected the daily lives of the blacks were local residents—the landowner and employer, the overseer, the man who ran the general store, village leaders and officials. Federal power had come from outside, from far away, and for virtually the first time, whereas the power of white southerners grew out of local realities and was long-standing and persistent. It was difficult for the federal government, operating through a limited number of appointed agents, to reach the newly freed blacks, who were embedded in the tightly knit web of local custom. It was practically impossible for the federal government to transform the conditions of life for the freedmen on an intimate and continuous basis. At certain points and certain times, the influence of the government could intervene in behalf of the former slaves, but in general their daily routine remained within the domain of the southerners.

The extent to which the slaves realized this circumstance emerges in an incident that involved a young black girl, the Ku Klux Klan, and the Yankees. The girl's family was struggling to make a better life for itself under severe Klan pressure in

Alabama. One night while her father was in hiding, white-robed men appeared at the cabin door and demanded to know where he was. As she fended off their questions, this girl recognized the voice of her father's former master, spoke with him, and coaxed him into admitting his identity. Soon after, the Yankees moved to suppress Klan outrages and brought many local whites to trial in Tuscaloosa. "Dey carried me [there too, and] . . . a man hel' me up an' made me p'int out who it was dat come to our house," reported the girl. Suddenly this black girl confronted a choice between sympathetic, but distant, Yankees and hostile, but ubiquitous, southerners. With canny foresight she pointed not to her former master but to a stranger. Then, looking directly at the former owner, she said, "'Dat's de man, ain't it Marster Will?'"[20] She had taken the situation in hand, choosing to let her master off the hook while ensuring that he realized what she had done.

Thus a guilty man escaped justice, and federal agents received no cooperation from someone whom they were trying to help. In another sense, however, this girl had wisely chosen the best alternative in a situation in which blacks remained at the mercy of local whites. If she had sent the master to jail, her family probably would have lost its farm and any hope of future employment in the area. The federal government would have been powerless to intervene. By shielding the former master, on the other hand, she protected her family's tenuous economic status and placed a powerful local white in her debt.

This appreciation of the continuing power of southern whites grew out of the entire past experience of the slaves, but it had also been bolstered by many recent actions by the whites. Some planters felt relief over the end of slavery and resolved to help their former dependents, but this reaction was not general. As the war came to an end thousands of masters demonstrated in unmistakable terms that they retained their hatred for blacks and were determined to keep them from rising in society. These masters had never wanted to give up slavery. Many of them attempted to keep it, either in the same form or with modifications, despite evidence on all sides that the war was bringing immense, revolutionary change.

Before the war had ended, untold numbers of slaveowners moved their slaves and other possessions to avoid the emancipation that accompanied advancing Union troops. In the upper South many who moved merely hoped to hold onto their slaves for as long as the Confederacy might last. But in the deep South, planters often intended to evade emancipation altogether, usually by moving to Texas, which had become a semiautonomous region under the Confederacy and might conceivably return to independent status someday. Cato Carter saw "folks leavin' for Texas" who said that "if the Fed'rals won the war they'd have to live in Texas to keep slaves. So plenty started driftin' their slaves to the west." Another former slave, who actually made the journey to Texas, remembered his master saying that "in Texas dere never be no freedom."[21]

Even after the southern armies surrendered, some masters tried to continue slavery by keeping the news from their bondsmen or refusing to let them go. After Will Sheets's mother announced that the slaves would be free, "Marse Jeff said us warn't, and he didn't tell us no diffunt 'till 'bout Chris'mas atter de War was done over wid in April." Another former slave said, "I hears 'bout freedom in September," when a government agent rode up to the farm and asked "why ain't massa turn the niggers loose." Others reported that their owners "didn't tell them it was freedom" or "wouldn't let [them] go." The reach of the federal government was far from complete. One officer in the Freedmen's Bureau confirmed such stories of continued bondage when he reported to his superiors that "I find the old system of slavery working with even more rigor than formerly at a few miles distant from any point where U.S. troops are stationed."[22]

Believing that they were entitled at least to some form of compensation, some slaveowners attempted to gain a lifetime lease on their property or the right to hold all slave children until they were twenty-one. One mistress "called all the children together to tell them that, even though they were free, they would have to remain with her" until maturity. The Freedmen's Bureau in Georgia found this ploy to be so common that it issued regulations affirming that parents had control of their children and allowing masters to become the guardians of minors only when these children had no family. Soon the white-controlled legislature passed a bill requiring that black orphans be apprenticed to a white man, and other states passed similar statutes, which were open to abuse. A woman who had experienced slavery in Mississippi said that after the war there, "all the orphans were taken and given back to the people that owned them when freedom came." She had two cousins who had to stay with their master "until they were twenty years old. . . . They wouldn't give them any schooling at all."[23]

Thus, with a variety of motives and through a variety of methods, some masters struggled to prolong slavery. It seems clear that many were intent primarily on keeping their labor supply through the harvest, but it is equally clear that others had more in mind. The slave narratives suggest that these practices were widespread. Of 674 narratives that gave information on the master's actions at the close of the war, 117 (or 17 percent) indicated that the master had prolonged slavery in some manner. Sixty-six claimed that he had tried to keep the adults; fifteen reported that he had attempted to control the children; and thirty-six described deception in regard to the news of freedom.

The reactions of masters who acknowledged the arrival of freedom also sent telling messages to the slaves. Though some planters tried to adjust to reality, other whites who could not stave off freedom cursed its coming or reacted violently to the loss of their human property. Emancipation had a desolating effect on masters who could not conceive of a world in which despised bondsmen enjoyed equal status with the white race. In frustration and rage some slaveowners sought to vent their spleen verbally, while others turned destructive impulses toward themselves or the freedmen.

On the day of emancipation George King's master emphatically told his former servants that freedom did not mean that they were white and did not mean that they were equal. " 'You is free to live and free to die and free to go to de devil,' " said another angry planter who expressed the same frame of mind. A South Carolina planter emigrated to England, explaining that he "couldn't stay in a country with so many free negroes," and a landowner in Georgia gagged at the idea of a freed Negro wearing a starched shirt. Forbidding all discussion of freedom in their presence, some planters made it clear that the idea of emancipation was repugnant to them. It was not surprising that Reverend Garrison Frazier, who met with Sherman, professed a desire for blacks to live off by themselves, "for there is a prejudice against us in the South that will take years to get over."[24]

This prejudice, when it could no longer find an outlet in domination of the slaves, sometimes turned inward and gnawed at the vitals of the former slaveowners. As the tide of events turned against the South, some masters turned to drink and tried to drown their awareness in a jug of whiskey. An owner in Texas grew increasingly morose, until he went " 'roun' sort of talkin' to hisse'f and den he [started] to cussin' ev'rybody." Within a year he moved away to separate himself from the freedmen he once controlled, but this separation brought no peace and he soon committed suicide. Another white "bent hisself over" when he heard of freedom "and never did straighten his body no more." Tom Wilson's master got "so mad 'bout hit he went off down to a li'l stream of water an' broke de ice an' jumped in, an' he died 'bout two weeks afte' of de pewmonia."[25] So many former slaves told of masters who died of apoplexy or gave up the will to live after emancipation that it seemed possible that various tales about the white people's anger had embroidered themselves into a legend. But these stories of the former slaves all differed in their particulars and gave distinguishing details, so they probably presented a valid picture of the effects of impotent rage. Independent studies based on white sources have confirmed that freeing the slaves was a profoundly traumatic experience for many planters.[26]

In some cases the masters directed their exasperation and hostility toward the slaves in the form of threats or actual violence. A South Carolinian called all of his slaves to the big house and showed them a sack of money that he had accumulated through owning them. Then he swore to kill them all before the Yankees set them free while he kept the money and the benefits of slavery. Other slaves told of masters who threatened to "free" their servants with a shotgun; Annie Row's owner took "de gun offen de rack and start[ed] for de field whar de niggers am a' workin,'" muttering, "Free de nigger, will dey? I free dem." A particularly cruel Virginia planter seized his pistol and fired into a crowd of field hands when he learned that none of them would stay through the harvest. In contrast, Ella Washington's master was cordial and ingratiating after news of freedom arrived. Within a day or two, however, the blacks started having cramps and dying, possibly because he had poisoned the well. The bitterness felt by some whites emerges in an incident described by two former slaves who had lived near Huntsville, Texas. As the newly emancipated slaves were celebrating their emancipation, "one gal was hollerin' loud and a white man come ridin' on a hoss and leans over and cut that gal nearly half in two." Similarly, a Georgia planter knocked down a woman who dared to sing about her imminent emancipation. Thus, the slaves faced a hostile world in which to begin their new lives.[27]

The most important decision that the freedmen confronted in the first days after the war was the choice of staying with the old master or leaving to seek their fortunes elsewhere. Many considerations entered into this choice, and some individuals had a unique reason for their action. But, overall the former slaves followed a consistent pattern that revealed their approach to freedom. Knowing that their liberation had not changed the hostile world, the blacks had to make a judgment as to where their chances of progress and liberty would be greatest. Drawing on their experiences in bondage, they tried to assess their former masters and compare them to other whites whom they might encounter. If their owner had been comparatively kind under slavery, they reasoned that he might allow them the most freedom after emancipation. A harsh slaveowner, on the other hand, represented a bad bet.

One former slave summarized his fellows' decisions in this manner: "Mos' all de Niggers dat had good owners stayed wid 'em, but de others lef'. Some of 'em come back an' some didn'." Adeline White, who had been in bondage to a cruel man in Louisiana, reported that most of the work force on her plantation left quickly, "for that massa am sho' mean and if we doesn't have to stay we shouldn't, not with that massa." In North Carolina a similarly situated group of slaves made the same choice. "An' lemmie tell yo'," said one of them, "we shore cussd ole marster out 'fore we left dar." On the other hand, a Georgian who had been good to his laborers and who offered to help them get a start in freedom found that most of his two hundred slaves refused to leave. Another wise planter eased the transition to a new order by rolling out two barrels of whiskey, killing a few hogs, and treating his former bondsmen to a grand celebration. Others supplied each black family with a mule, a cow, some tools, money, or even land and thus won the freedmen's goodwill.[28]

The first year represented the primary period of decision. Soldiers and runaways left during the war, and many who had endured a cruel owner left within a week or month. Others remained through that year's harvest and pondered their opportunities before deciding to go. Of those who chose to stay, a large number remained for several years, and a few went off briefly to taste their liberty before returning. There was a tendency for white interviewers to elicit more information about loyalty to a kind owner that kept the bondsmen from leaving With white interviewers half the former slaves reported leaving, whereas with black interviewers nearly two-thirds did so. Table 5.2 summarizes the information supplied about this decision.

Among reported reasons for these decisions, the freedmen gave the greatest weight to the character of their former master. As table 5.3 shows, nearly half of the former slaves who explained their decisions declared that they left harsh owners to seek a better future elsewhere or chose to stay and work for men who had proven to be relatively fair minded toward blacks. In the uncertain new world of freedom, known quantities carried great weight, and well-regarded masters had a great advantage in the labor market. The largest single group of former slaves indicated that favorable impressions of their masters induced them to stay and work on the plantation. One woman whose husband lived nearby faced a choice between working for her owners or leaving to join her husband. She refused to go with

Table 5.2   Decision to Stay with or Leave Master after Freedom

Decision	Percentage	Number
Left during war	5.5	87
Left immediately	9.0	142
Left within a month	9.2	145
Left within a year	18.8	297
Left, time uncertain	9.6	152
Stayed one to two years	4.7	74
Stayed three to five years	10.2	161
Stayed several years or more	22.1	350
Stayed, time uncertain	9.6	152
Left but returned	1.5	22
Total	100.2	1582

Table 5.3   Reported Reasons for Staying or Leaving

Reason	Percentage	Number
Left to join United States Army	3.2	24
Left to reunite family	20.4	152
Left because disliked master	19.0	141
Left to seek opportunity	3.9	29
Left to marry	2.1	16
Master forced them to leave	2.1	16
Left to rejoin good master	0.5	4
Left, other reason	1.5	11
Liked master, stayed	27.8	207
Had good job, stayed	3.8	28
No alternative, stayed	4.0	30
Stayed for promised reward	0.7	5
Kept by master	0.7	5
Stayed, other reason	0.5	4
Circumstances forced decision	9.8	73
Total	100.0	745

him, saying, "I knowed my white folks and they was good to me, but I didn't know his white folks."[29]

After an assessment of the master, the desire to reunite with one's family had the greatest influence over the freedmen's decisions. Some forced marriages dating from slavery broke up at the end of the war as the individuals involved sought separate lives more in tune with their own preferences. In many more cases men and women who had endured years of separation embarked on inspired searches for their loved ones. Traveling on foot, often with only vague information about a relative's location, thousands of blacks persisted in quests that would have been quixotic but for the fact that they often proved successful.[30] The black community united in extending its aid to such people, and small hints and bits of news eventually drew many broken families together again perhaps one, two, or even more years after freedom. Table 5.3 shows that, next to the perceptions of one's master, the desire to reunite a family was the most important factor in decisions about staying on or leaving the plantation.

The past occupations of freedmen had some influence on the likelihood that they would be "loyal" to their former owner instead of leaving him to seek a brighter destiny elsewhere. As table 5.4 indicates, house servants were somewhat more inclined to remain with their master than were field hands or artisans. This relationship is quite weak, however, and past treatment had a stronger effect on the slaves' actions. Tables 5.5, 5.6, and 5.7 set forth the relationship between the decision to stay or go and three factors connected with treatment: the slaves' attitude toward the master, the food they had received, and the master's actions at the end of the war. In each case the relationship is stronger. The freedmen's actions varied considerably in accord with the opinions that they held of their masters and the food they had received. There was also a clear relationship between the master's action at the war's end and the decisions of the freedmen. Taken together, these four tables show that, rather than dividing along occupational lines, the slave community

Table 5.4   Occupation in Slavery and Decision to Stay or Leave
(Gamma = −.175)

| Occupation | Percentage | | | Number |
	Left within One Year	Stayed 1-2 Years	Stayed 3 Years or More	
House servant	52.4	5.1	42.5	332
Field hand	60.1	8.7	31.2	218
Artisan	60.0	13.3	26.7	15
Total				565

Table 5.5 Attitude toward Master and Decision to Stay or Leave
(Gamma = −.498)

Attitude	Percentage			Number
	Left within One Year	Stayed 1–2 Years	Stayed 3 Years or More	
Very favorable	32.6	7.0	60.5	86
Favorable	45.2	7.3	47.5	562
Unfavorable	74.0	3.4	22.6	208
Very unfavorable	80.4	4.1	15.5	97
Total				953

Table 5.6 Ratings of Food and Decision to Stay or Leave
(Gamma = −.359)

Ratings	Percentage			Number
	Left within One Year	Stayed 1–2 Years	Stayed 3 Years or More	
Same as master's	46.8	6.4	46.8	47
Good	45.8	7.4	46.7	443
Adequate	63.2	3.9	32.9	76
Inadequate	75.3	6.2	18.5	81
Bad	84.6	7.7	7.7	13
Total				660

Table 5.7 Master's Action at End of War and Decision to Stay or Leave
(Gamma = .436)

| Master's Action | Percentage | | | Number |
	Left within One Year	Stayed 1–2 Years	Stayed 3 Years or More	
Told slaves to leave	81.5	7.4	11.1	27
Delayed telling of freedom or tried to keep in slavery	69.1	4.1	26.8	97
Offered jobs	42.7	8.2	49.1	171
Gave aid	34.9	5.8	59.3	86
Total				381

basically responded as a unit to the treatment experienced under various masters and the resulting perceptions of the amount of opportunity likely to exist under these men as employers.[31]

While some stayed, many freedmen decided to leave their plantation and search for brighter opportunities elsewhere. White observers, often stricken with fear that the area's agricultural labor force would disappear, frequently charged that the blacks were moving about mindlessly and irresponsibly without regard for the future. The principle of unrestricted movement was indeed important to the former slaves, for they wanted to enjoy all the privileges of free men. To explain why some blacks "started on the move," one man observed that "they seemed to want to get closer to freedom, so they'd know what it was—like it was a place or a city." Another informant recalled that he had sung a song about being free as a frog, "'cause a frog had freedom to git on a log and jump off when he pleases."[32] Movement was an integral part of the freedmen's testing of their environment, their examination of the boundaries of the postwar world. After years of slavery, they sought to move cautiously ahead and improve their lives. During Reconstruction blacks would push steadily against those boundaries, trying to enlarge the area·of freedom and secure as many gains for themselves as they could.

6.

"Starting Uphill, den Going Back"

Initially, southern blacks moved with shrewdness and caution into the world of freedom. Carefully, almost instinctively, they picked their way toward full lives in freedom. While aware of the limits on their opportunity, they sought to maximize whatever advantages were possible. Without abandoning these tactics, the freedmen soon adopted greater boldness, however, and pinned their hopes for full freedom on the northern attempt to remake southern society. Their actions represented a decision to take substantial risks amid known dangers and demonstrated the depth of their desire for meaningful change. Their courage during Reconstruction also showed that slavery had not rendered them psychologically impotent or dependent upon their masters.

In the end, of course, Reconstruction brought tragedy to southern blacks. Time proved that they had taken great risks only to suffer great loss. Their northern allies failed them, and the hostility of southern whites remained strong. Thus, their underlying, initial assumptions sadly proved correct. But in the process the former slaves had secured many small but meaningful gains for their families and for their social and cultural life. They retained the will to struggle for full freedom in the future.

From the first days of freedom, blacks began to insist on the dividends of their emancipation and to demand that the old order of bondage change. As in their resistance to slavery, they concentrated first on the mundane but vital issues of life and endeavored to win a greater area of personal autonomy, protection for their families, and better treatment for themselves. Some, like Tempie Cummins's mother, sabotaged the master's hopes of keeping slavery a bit longer by joyously spreading the news of freedom. That night Tempie's mother slipped back to the quarters and spirited her daughter away despite the master's surveillance. Similarly, other freedmen moved to protect the integrity of their families. Saying, "You took her away from me an' didn' pay no mind to my cryin', so now I'se takin' her back home," the mother of Sarah Debro reclaimed a child whom the mistress had been raising in her own home. Another woman reacted to orders to get to work at the spinning wheel by declaring, "I ain't gwineter, I'm jest as free as you air [are]" and then packing up her family and moving away. When she heard that her former master intended to pay nothing but food and clothing after the war, Ann Evans spoke right up and said, "Why boss, dey tells me dat since freedom we git a little change."[1]

Unshackled from bondage, the freedmen insisted that the physical abuse of slavery end. Alex Pope's master told the adults that he no longer had the right to whip them but that he "would brush dey chilluns if dey didn't do right." Straightaway Alex's mother informed him that "he warn't gwine brush none of her chilluns no more." Rhody Holsell recalled that once after freedom was declared the mistress struck her, but "I grabbed her leg and would have broke her neck." After Rhody had thus clarified the ground rules of freedom, the mistress tried to apologize, but the former slave would not let her. As one man put it, the blacks were tired of punishment and after freedom "day sho' didn't take no more foolishment off of white folks." An individual who worked on riverboats after the war explained that fights frequently broke out if the mate became too mean, because "the Negroes had only a few years of freedom and resented cruelty."[2]

As we have seen, many former slaves decided that conditions on their plantation allowed them too little scope and sought greater opportunities in a new setting. Despite the fears of many planters that their entire labor source would abandon the region, the narratives suggest that most freedmen who left their old master moved somewhere close by. On a neighboring plantation or not too far distant, they could join family members or pursue greater opportunity with an employer who enjoyed a favorable reputation or had reacted helpfully to emancipation. Here again most of the slaves were cautiously but alertly searching for ways to maximize the advantages of freedom. Table 6.1 indicates the destinations of those who left their plantation and moved elsewhere.

Table 6.1   Destinations of Migrants

Destination	Percentage	Number
Nearby in same state	63.3	614
Far in same state	1.8	17
New state	19.8	192
From farm to town	15.2	147
Total	100.1	970

Rural migrations were difficult for southern planters to follow, but aggregations of former slaves were especially noticeable in the cities. There the freedmen found a new pattern of life and greater opportunities for social contact with each other. Urban life was rewarding for some, such as a woman who recalled that there was "a big bunch of us niggers in town and we [were] stirrin' 'round like bees workin' in and out a hive." A few achieved prosperity and, in Amanda McCray's words, "blossomed out with fine phaetons (buggies) and ceiled houses, and clothes—oh my!" Another former slave attributed this gaudy display to "a sort of reaction from the restraint upon them in slavery." But times were hard in the war-torn South, and most encountered hunger and sickness in the cities. Tom W. Neal remembered that the freedmen were sleeping "anywhere they could find" and relying on United States rations while "hunt[ing] work." Liney Chambers added, and traditional sources confirm, that "diseases and changing ways of eatin' and livin'" led to "consumption and fevers" from which many died. Exposure to a wider range of illnesses, crowded living conditions, and inadequate medical care or the denial of medical facilities also contributed to sickness among urban dwellers.[3]

Although the fears of planters were probably overdrawn, many freedmen who migrated within rural areas did in fact leave their state and move to another. Close to 85 percent of the former slaves in the narratives stayed within their state during Reconstruction, but some of the remainder reported long journeys to new regions in the South.[4] The lands on the southern frontier acted as a magnet, drawing freedmen westward just as they had drawn many whites. Arkansas and Texas had entered into a phase of rapid development, and opportunity seemed bright there in comparison to some of the older areas of the upper South or border states. The greatest amount of reported outmigration was from Virginia, with Kentucky and Tennessee not far behind. Apparently many freedmen who lived in Alabama and Mississippi, which recently had been on the frontier, decided that the future lay still further west, for they also moved away in substantial numbers. Almost half of the migrants reported that their destination had been Arkansas or Texas, and although a few western states ranked next, no other state received any substantial portion of the migrants.

Perhaps some of these migrants found a promised land at the end of their journeys, but most probably did not; for, in general, times were also hard for rural blacks at the beginning of Reconstruction. One former slave humorously remarked that "nigh 'bout ever' nigger in de world cussed ole Abraham Lincoln dat [first] winter," and John Love gave thanks that there were "plenty wild animals" that could be hunted for food. "Money was scarce and our feedin' was pore," agreed another former slave, and some believed that the first years of freedom were harder than the Great Depression. But there was a difference from slavery, one which the freedmen appreciated. Lewis Bon-

Table 6.2   Outmigration Rates during Reconstruction—Selected States

State	Percentage Who Left	Percentage Who Stayed	Number of Migrants	Total Reporting
Virginia	33.6	66.4	37	110
Kentucky	31.0	69.0	18	58
Alabama	24.0	76.0	31	129
Tennessee	18.7	81.3	25	134
Mississippi	18.2	81.8	29	159
Missouri	17.9	82.1	10	56
Georgia	17.0	83.0	37	218
North Carolina	11.3	88.7	20	177
South Carolina	9.1	90.9	21	231
Texas	5.1	94.9	10	198

Table 6.3   Reported Destinations of Migrants—Selected States

State	Percentage of Migrants	Numer of Migrants
Arkansas	28.3	78
Texas	17.4	48
Mississippi	9.0	25
Tennessee	6.2	17
Alabama	5.4	15
Georgia	4.7	13
Louisiana	4.7	13
Ohio	4.3	12
Indiana	2.9	8
Kentucky	2.5	7
Total	85.4	236

ner, who sharecropped with his old master in Texas for three years, admitted that he earned little money, but pointed out that he "got room and board and didn't have to work too hard. It was enough difference to tell you was no slaves any more."[5]

Along with survival, a high priority in these early years of freedom was the desire to achieve a greater insulation of black family and social life from white interference. Though freedom had not eliminated white hostility, it at least had brought a measure of independence, enough to allow blacks to shield the private areas of their lives from white intrusion and supervision. Families used freedom to reunite and build a better life away from the dependence and surveillance of the slave quarters. "After the war my stepfather come and got my mother and we moved out in the piney woods," said Annie Young, voicing a theme common to many of the narratives. Others spoke of moving "across de creek to [themselves]" or building a "saplin house . . . back in de woods" or " 'way off in de woods." Even when blacks stayed on the same land, they might establish new residences in a different section of the property. Many rural freedmen moved into small all-black settlements, which still exist along some of the South's backroads today. Thus, the newly freed slaves showed a general preference for living in independent fashion by themselves.[6]

The value of independence even led some privileged house servants to place distance between themselves and the master and pass up advantages offered by the whites. After moving his family to a shack in Freetown, one man turned down the master's offer of the overseer's house to live in and declined to let the former owner grind his grain for free. He preferred to pay one-eighth of the grain elsewhere because "it made him feel like a free man to pay fo' things jus' like anyone else." Louisa Collier's parents had been the carriage driver and a trusted house servant to the master, but after the war they moved "in de colored settle-ment and den [they] ain' eat at de big house no more neither."

A few of the more perceptive and broad-minded owners recognized this desire among the former slaves and facilitated the establishment of separate dwellings as a means of keeping their workers. One North Carolinian gave his former slaves the opportunity to build houses on a nearby plantation that he owned if they would stay, and other planters permitted the blacks to build new log cabins away from the quarters. [7]

As part of this desire to protect their family and social life, the newly freed southerners established their own black churches. Through the dark years of bondage, separate religious meetings had necessarily been secret, but now the freedmen could worship as they chose in the open. Many former slaves, like John Davenport, reported that "atter de war, some of de niggers started a brush arbor." These brush arbors, "a sort of . . . shelter with leaves for a roof," were all that the freedmen could afford to build at first, but the rudeness of the surroundings did not keep them from glorifying their God. "Preachin' and shouting sometimes lasted all day Sundays," recalled one informant, and another spoke of "de glorious times den" when the blacks could worship together in freedom. [8]

Another characteristic part of the slaves' response to freedom was a fervent and nearly universal interest in education. Long denied the key to knowledge, the freedmen wanted to break out of their ignorance and learn to read and write. Sitting on "log seats" or "a dirt flo'," they started learning their lessons after the war. Men and women often couldn't attend school until "de crops was laid by," but at least some of the children were able to go "all de time." Even "old, old slaves" tried to learn to read, though the new scholars might have only old almanacs, discarded novels, or disintegrating dictionaries for texts. One indication of the depth of desire for education was the fact that many former slaves reported paying tuition, typically a dollar a month, for their schooling. This amount represented a sizeable chunk out of many families' income in the postwar years. Yet, the relatively few blacks who had been able to obtain an education found no shortage of pupils when they opened their own schools.[9]

Although blacks made great gains in literacy during Reconstruction, inevitably there were many individuals who had to drop out of school to help their parents in the fields or who never had a school in their area. Years later these former slaves bemoaned their own ignorance but usually pointed with pride to the academic accomplishments of their children. "I has four young'uns and every one of dem had schoolin' and larnin'," said one woman. Another explained that she had made sacrifices for her children's education because "I don't want dem to be like dey mammy, a unknowledge person."[10]

Along with education, the freedmen had a strong desire for land. For a fortunate few land and the chance for real progress that it brought came as a gift from a sympathetic master. In most cases, however, this was not true, and sometimes community pressure opposed even the renting of land to blacks. In Georgia Mrs. Charles Colcock Jones was outraged over the fact that two landowners planned to "rent their lands to the Negroes!" Other southerners shared her belief that such action was "very injurious to the best interest of the community." As Elige Davison observed, "Mos' niggers jus' got turn loose with a cuss and not 'nough clothes to cover they bodies." For the great majority land had to be obtained in some other way. Occasionally, some freedmen tried to claim and keep part of the land that they had been working all their lives, but local whites and federal officials put an end to such attempts. Thus, the major hope for land rested with the United States Congress and proposals of forty acres and a mule. A few former slaves denied that they had heard of these proposals, but many more reported that they had heard "a heap o' talk" on the subject from "Yankees" or "speakers gwine aroun'." John Hunter in North Carolina had heard "that the President and the Governor was going to give land to the niggers—going to take it off the owners that they worked for," and Sam McAllum in Mississippi had believed the stories and "picked out [his] mule." "All o' us did," he said. The faith in a division of land was so great that some slaves invented a song about Uncle Sam giving "us all a farm" and others fell prey to crooks who "sold" sections of the slaveowners' land.[11]

Forced by necessity to labor on for the planters, freedmen found themselves in frequent controversy over the terms of their employment. When an Alabama freedman refused to sign an objectionable labor contract in 1867, his former master threatened him, forcing the black man to draw a pistol in defense and then leave the farm for good. Such arguments over the terms of labor sometimes improved the freedmen's position, however. Shade Richards explained that at first some landowners gave the sharecroppers only a tenth of what they raised, but there ensued a "lot of mouthin' about it" and the proportion then rose first to a third and later to a half. A recent study has documented that this kind of process aided Alabama freedmen during the first years of Reconstruction. If argument with the landowner produced no results, freedmen could move elsewhere in hopes of better treatment or could appeal to federal authorities. Cheated by her former owner in Florida, Mary Biddle mounted a mule and rode to the nearest Union garrison, where federal troops gave her a letter reminding the employer of his obligations. Another former slave from Kentucky reported success in a similar situation, but appealing to the Northern troops often involved substantial costs. Mary Biddle had to leave her farm and seek a new employer, and the former slave in Kentucky had to "put herself under the protection of the police until we could get away."[12]

These two incidents highlighted the risk involved in placing one's reliance on the federal government and the new order that it promised in the South. Through steady pressure and watchful waiting, blacks could secure a few modest but meaningful gains from their former owners. Greater progress required the intervention of the northerners, but this was certain to arouse the ire of local whites who were determined to maintain existing patterns of status and authority. Aware of the prejudice among all whites and familiar with the persisting power of southern planters, the freedmen took a great chance when they cast their lot with the Yankees. In this context, the decision of thousands of southern blacks to vote, and to vote Republican, takes on new meaning. To participate in the new political system mandated by military Reconstruction was to alienate white southerners, who still had major influence over the freedmen's lives. By going to the polls and electing Republican governments, the slaves were leaving caution behind to gamble on a brighter future. Undoubtedly they took this step in the sobering knowledge that if their gamble failed, they would again find themselves at the mercy of the embittered men who once owned them.

Nevertheless, the great majority of blacks lined up on the Republican side. Remembering their days as voters, the former slaves told how they refused bribes and pressures to vote against the party to which they owed their loyalty for emancipation. "I sticks out to de end wid de party dat freed me," said Bill McNeil, voicing the sentiments of many others. Some who came under severe pressure to vote Democratic "would take pay for voting and then vote different, [although] when the night riders found it out, there would be trouble." William Henry could read only "a little," but he and other blacks had no trouble identifying the Republican ballot: "We stood around and watched. We saw D. Sledge vote; he owned half of the county. We knowed he voted Democrat so we voted the other ticket so it would be Republican."[13]

Parades, rousing political songs, and other devices helped to cement this loyalty to the party of Lincoln. In some areas the Republicans had organized Loyal Leagues or other clubs to educate and protect black voters. The narratives also confirm that black ministers and women played a large role in political decision making. When Franklin Moses was running for governor in South Carolina, preachers had a ready-made text on Moses leading his people out of the wilderness. In other states meetings at the church also included political advice. Some preachers exhorted the women "to have nothin' to do wid deir husbands" if they didn't vote right, and one man lamented that after he gave in to Klan pressure, "my wife wouldn't sleep wid me for six months." Another former slave reported that during one campaign the "colored preachers so 'furiate de women, dat they would put on breeches and vote de 'Publican radical ticket."[14]

To counter the Republican influence, southern Democrats relied on several different methods. In addition to economic coercion and the threat of violence, they sometimes resorted to tricks designed to humiliate the freedmen and disrupt their political activities. Before one Republican meeting in South Carolina, the Democrats arranged for a local merchant to furnish the freedmen with some fine whiskey. The liquor had been doctored with a fast-acting laxative, however, and few of the men were well enough to attend their meeting. Another former slave reported that in his town local whites invented a ruse that allowed them to steal the blacks' registration forms just before an election and thus weaken Republican strength at the polls.[15]

The narratives are virtually unanimous in their praise of the Republicans during Reconstruction. Not a single black interviewer heard from a freedman who voted Democratic, and eighteen of the twenty-five former slaves who claimed to have been Democrats were from one state, South Carolina, in which pressures at the time of the interview may have been particularly strong. Analysis of the backgrounds of those who professed Democratic loyalty indicated that they were more likely than their Republican counterparts to have been house servants and to have stayed on with the master for several years or more. Apparently such backgrounds inclined them either to vote with the whites or to give the interviewer answers that pleased him. It is clear that on the whole, despite a variety of pressures and tricks, the Democrats were not able to obtain many black votes before the end of Reconstruction.[16]

Nevertheless, voting entailed very real dangers for the freedmen, who sensed the enduring weakness of the Republican party among powerful southerners. The white boycott of the polls in many states drew the line of allegiance quite clearly and made the exercise of suffrage by blacks an act of defiance to the local white community. "In dem days nobody but Niggers an' shawl-strop folks [carpetbaggers] voted," recalled Charlie Davenport. "It was powerful ticklish times," he added, "an' I let votin' alone." Another former slave described the Republicans as "some strange folks and trashy niggers and po' white folks dat ain't never had nothing." His language plainly was couched in accommodationist terms; yet he made a valid point. Leading Republicans were in many cases either outsiders or less impressive and less perceptibly powerful people than the former slaveowners. It was not always possible to circumvent the ingrained local power structure, as Jesse Williams made clear when he described the trial of a white terrorist in South Carolina. The judge had to find the defendant guilty due to the overwhelming weight of the evidence, but using his discretion this jurist imposed a fine of only one dollar, to the cheers and celebration of the local populace. Yet, many blacks fought to bring a new political order to the South. The narratives also contain accounts of violent political encounters, such as the murder in 1875 in South Carolina of Joe Crews, a white organizer of the black militia, and the Brooks-Baxter War, which ended Reconstruction in Arkansas.[17]

Eventually, of course, as northern support for Reconstruction declined, intransigent southerners prevailed with the aid of the Ku Klux Klan, and the narratives contain many comments on this terrorist organization. A few former slaves suggested that an organization known as the Ku Klux existed before the war and that the word *Klan* was not part of its title. "The Ku Klux in slavery times," explained Joseph Badgett, "were men who would catch Negroes out and keep them if they did not collect [a ransom] from their masters." Some interviewers, particularly in Arkansas, repeatedly encountered this insistence that the Ku Klux was prewar, and Gladys-Marie Fry has recently argued that the Klan may in fact have derived its name from a branch of the Catawba Indians, whose relations with blacks had been generally hostile. Additional confusion about the Klan arose from the fact that in many parts of the South the old system of patrols apparently did not stop after the Civil War, and former slaves frequently spoke of "paddyroles [who] were very active after freedom." Whatever the background of the Klan, however, many former slaves made clear that they had not been fooled by the Klansmen's ghostly attire. In fact, many freedmen recognized the nightriders by their horses, stature, and voices; for the Klansmen often were familiar white men, such as a former owner or his relatives. After a short while the former slaves became familiar with the nightriders' tricks (for example, "drinking" great quantities of water that actually went into a rubber bag) and learned to distinguish between various aims of the terrorists.[18]

In part the Klan's purpose was political. Several informants testified that nightriders had warned them to vote Democratic or whipped them for listening to carpetbaggers and scalawags. One woman reported that the Klan threatened to seize her uncle if he voted Republican. Mack Taylor said, "I was given a warnin' once, to watch my step and vote right." Klansmen told another man that they would "whale de devil out of him" if he did not stop listening to scalawags and carpetbaggers. When a South Carolina scalawag started employing blacks and bringing them to the polls to vote Republican, nightriders promptly visited his plantation and "whipped every nigger man they could lay deir hands on." Another way to interfere with black political activity was to break up their club meetings. Such incidents sometimes resulted in violence and death.[19]

But the narratives suggest that white terrorism also served as an important means of labor control; indeed, this seemed to be the earliest purpose of the Klan in some areas. Klansmen told John Wesley that "they wanted folks to stay at home and work." Other former slaves received whippings "for doin' too much visitin' " or for letting grass grow up among the crops. William Watkins reported that in Charlotte County, Virginia, the Klan appeared "right after de war" and went to work whipping "de slaves what leaves de plantations." A Texas freedman recalled that wages were so low and pay so irregular in 1868 that "if it hadn't been for them there Klu Klux, . . . the niggers would have went on the warpath for starvin'. But the Klu Kluxers wouldn't let 'em roam none, [and] if they tried they stretch them out over a log and hit them with rawhide." Similarly, Lorenza Ezell, who had been a slave in South Carolina, recalled that the first wave of the Klan concentrated on driving the freedmen back to their old farms. In these nocturnal forays, some freedmen recognized their former masters' voices and conversed openly with them about their identity ("Sho, it's me," said one planter. "Whar's yo' daddy?") Later the Klan adopted political goals or sought to suppress manifestations of a desire for equality among the blacks. Schools with Yankee teachers and blacks who had prospered became targets, along with any freedman who asserted himself too forcefully. Selie Anderson, for example, reported that some whites killed her uncle because he had argued with them over a bridle. Table 6.4 summarizes the variety of goals that appeared in Klan activities described by the former slaves.[20]

Table 6.4   Reports on the Klan's Purpose

Purpose	Percentage	Number
To control politics	33.1	43
To control the labor force	23.8	31
To control status and attitudes	26.9	35
Financial gain	7.7	10
To stop education	3.8	5
Other	4.6	6
Total	99.9	130

To fight this terrorism the blacks could rely on a local white or on United States authorities for protection, but the slave narratives tell most often of blacks who met violence with violence and resisted the Klan directly. Former slaves told of men in Louisiana, Alabama, Kentucky, and other states who armed themselves and killed Klansmen who had attacked them. One of these individuals, after having to watch nightriders butcher his wife, begged for permission to get a sheet in which to wrap her body. Returning with a Winchester instead, he killed fourteen of the Klansmen. Another black learned that Klansmen were coming after him and concealed himself in the woods with some firearms. When the terrorists approached, he "open[ed] fire and kilt seven of them." Near Enfield, North Carolina, the efforts of a group of young blacks to defend themselves proved successful. After these freedmen planned and laid an ambush, the whites "got wind of it and stopped coming." James Stith reported that in Georgia in 1869 and 1870 the freedmen tied ropes and vines across the roads at night, as they had once done against the patrollers.[21]

As these last examples suggest, determined freedmen sometimes went so far as to organize paramilitary units for self-defense. In Macon, Georgia, a group of blacks organized what Berry Clay described as

a military clan . . . for the purpose of giving the ex-slaves a knowledge of drilling and war tactics. An order to disband was received from the "Black Horse Calvery [*sic*]" by the leader of the group. His life was threatened when he failed to obey so he prepared for a surprise visit. He fortified his house with twenty-five men on the inside and the same number outside. When the approaching calvarymen [*sic*] reached a certain point, the fifty hidden men fired at the same time. Seven members of the band were killed and many others wounded. There was no further interference from this group.

Similar military organizations in South Carolina, Mississippi, Texas, and North Carolina are also described. Apparently their leaders often had experience in the army, and these bands sometimes met in local black institutions such as the African Methodist Episcopal Church. In all, the narratives recount at least five pitched battles between such groups and the Klan. "A lot of them Ku Kluxes" were killed, said Pierce Harper, as black men defended their rights.[22]

Yet, in one case after another, reports of resistance ended with the information that the black resisters had to flee the area or go into hiding. The balance of power weighed heavily against the freedmen, and in time the more numerous and powerful whites prevailed. The very openness of some Klan activities testified to the assurance of its members; former slaves who knew the Klansmen's plans reported that they weren't harmed because "dey knowed I warnt gwine tell."[23] In short, white power was too pervasive for individuals or a disadvantaged minority to challenge successfully. The outcome of Reconstruction confirmed blacks' worst fears and the wisdom of their initial caution. "Atter de war," said Nellie Lloyd, who summarized a collective tragedy, "de niggers started up hill; den went back."[24] After so-called Redemption the freedmen faced heavy odds as they labored to make progress with little to support them but their families and their religion.

7.

Life Patterns of the Freedom Generation

When black progress slowed and "den went back" again, society fastened cruel constraints on the destiny of millions of southern freedmen. The failure of Reconstruction doomed the former slaves to lives stunted by the effects of caste and color prejudice. Instead of the legendary opportunity to rise to the limit of one's abilities, America offered black people a second-class citizenship that soon withered further before political exclusion and social segregation. Under the control of the Redeemers, the South first crippled and then eliminated many essential rights of black citizens, returning them to a role little different from slavery. This is a tragic and saddening story, which historians have been telling with accuracy and care in recent years.

The slave narratives provide a black perspective on these depressing events, but they do much more besides. In the life histories of the former slaves there is another story, a story of personal triumphs in the face of social defeats. Despite the limitations that America imposed, thousands of freedmen shaped rewarding lives for themselves based upon family and religion. Faith and fidelity, endurance and love, were the foundation stones upon which many built lives of honor and personal achievement in a forbidding environment. Oppression robbed southern blacks of a real opportunity for material progress, but such oppression could not eradicate their humanity. One's central challenge, as Judge Learned Hand once observed, is to be a success as a human being, and large numbers of the freedmen rose to that challenge in spite of everything else.

Promising more than it delivered and raising hopes that it

left unfulfilled, Reconstruction was a monumental disappointment for black southerners. For a few years Congress allowed them to enjoy political rights, but without an economic foundation on which they could rely few were able to maintain their independence against the varied pressures of a prejudiced society. As they looked back on their experiences, some of the former slaves proved to be perspicacious critics of postwar Republican policies. Thomas Hall, for example, asked whether Lincoln had in fact freed the slaves. "He give us freedom without giving us any chance to live to ourselves and we still had to depend on the southern white man for work, food and clothing," Hall explained. This economic dependence on the white man was fatal, Hall emphasized, because "he held us through our necessity and want in a state of servitude but little better than slavery." Putting the matter more simply, Harriet Davis remarked that "Lincoln was a fine conscientious man . . . but he turned us out without anything to eat or live on."[1]

Most federal programs that held out the promise of land—such as seizure and sale of land under the direct tax act, Sherman's Special Field Order Number 15, and proposals for confiscation—had been curtailed, reversed, or defeated, but a few blacks did try to locate on unsettled public lands. For them the venture was usually unsuccessful. James Lucas told interviewers that after his discharge from the army the government gave him 160 acres in Arkansas. But the land was uncleared, low, and swampy, and Lucas asked, "How I gwine-a dreen an' clear a lot o' lan' wid nothin' to do it wid? Reckon somebody livin' on my lan' now." Overall, the opportunities for economic advancement proved to be far more illusory than real. Using a striking image, Patsy Mitchner compared slavery and freedom to two snakes, each "full of pisen," one lying "wid his head pintin' north, de other wid his head pintin' south." Slavery had been "a bad thing," she allowed, but freedom "of de kin' we got wid nothin' to live on wus bad [too]. . . . Both bit de nigger, an' dey wus both bad."[2]

As the former slaves recounted their lives in freedom, it was evident that for some the conditions of daily life changed hardly at all. Through legal and extralegal means, some masters managed to continue their dominance over people who had once been their property. Because his mother could not find adequate work, Samuel Watson had been indentured to a planter in Kentucky. For eighteen years he served this man, whom he called master; five times he was whipped; and as the term of service drew to a close, the planter refused to provide the education, horse, and clothes that had been specified in the original contract. Ultimately, through a lawsuit Watson won $115 as final settlement for his services. Others reported that the social controls of slavery sometimes remained in force after the war. Joseph Badgett recalled that in Dallas County, Arkansas, blacks had to use the term *master* until after 1869 or 1870, and everyone had to obtain permission, if not an actual pass, from "the 'white folks' " before going anywhere. Apparently patrollers still crisscrossed the roads in some districts long after freedom.[3]

Beyond such overt signs of oppression, there extended a more pervasive and continual threat of violence. The Klan or other groups of whites sometimes attacked the "uppity" and aggressive blacks who were pressing for change. In South Carolina in 1878 Democrats shot a freedman who was trying to help another black cast a Republican ballot. This man was challenging the structure of power, but no one was safe from random displays of white dominance. A few years after Reconstruction, one woman in Texas lost her husband because he had inadvertently angered a white man. Only recently married, this couple was walking down the street when "Rufus accident'ly steps on a white man's foot and de white man kills him with a pistol." In Arkansas a black visitor from out of town mistakenly walked into the lobby of a white hotel. He backed out immediately in fright, but angry men killed him anyway. Such incidents, occurring from time to time across the South, spread fear throughout the black community, fear that the practice of lynching soon intensified.[4]

For the thousands who were not murdered or coerced into a perpetuation of slavery, life as landless agricultural laborers offered a few areas of improvement. "Dey have plantations and overseers like slavery," said William Stone, "but most de overseers niggers, and dey didn't whip you den." "Things was jus' the same . . . ," added Bert Strong, "only they got a little money." Undoubtedly the majority of freedmen, who had deeply resented physical abuse, agreed with Rosa Washington that conditions were "better since [the] war" because there were "no whippin's goin' on like they did 'fore."[5]

Economically, however, the dividends of freedom were disappointing. Through a variety of means landowners usually profited while their tenants and sharecroppers struggled along at subsistence level or in debt. Most shared the experience of Manda Walker's husband: "After de last bale was sold, every year, him come home wid de same sick smile and de same sad tale: 'Well, Mandy, as usual, I settled up and it was—"Naught is naught and figger is a figger, all for de white man and none for de nigger." ' " Although at first relatively few were able to obtain the land that would enable them to break out of the vicious cycles of sharecropping and the crop lien, over the years a larger number of blacks succeeded in purchasing land.[6] At the time of their interviews, approximately 10 percent of the former slaves were landowners, with holdings ranging from a small city lot to almost one thousand acres, the typical case being a small homestead. Other informants indicated that they had owned property but lost it when the depression struck.

In an attempt to better their conditions, many of the former slaves had moved from one state to another in the decades since the 1870s. As one might expect from the longer span of time, the proportion of migrants was higher than it had been during Reconstruction. In all, one-third of the former slaves who supplied information had ended up in a different state. Their pattern of movement showed a few variations from the earlier period, but the similarities were more striking. The former slaves had continued to migrate away from the upper South, border states, and cotton areas just east of the Mississippi River and had headed west, primarily to Arkansas, Texas, or Oklahoma. A few had drifted north, but the great exodus to northern cities affected younger generations far more than it did those who had experienced slavery.

The old-timers, however, had felt some of the impact of economic change as the South began to develop railroads, extractive industries, and other elements of a modern diversified economy. Almost two-thirds of the men and one-third of the women indicated that they had farmed for a living at some point, but a substantial portion of the men described some branch of industry or industrial labor as their primary occupation. Many had labored on railroads or in mines and sawmills and had thus helped to change the region. Black jobs customarily were the dirty and heavy jobs, and the former slaves as a group remained near the bottom of the economic ladder. It was especially notice-

Table 7.1   *Reported Outmigration after Reconstruction—Selected States*

State	Percentage Who Left	Percentage Who Stayed	Number of Migrants	Total Reporting
Mississippi	88.0	12.0	139	158
Kentucky	70.2	29.8	33	47
Tennessee	62.2	37.8	79	127
Alabama	48.2	51.8	55	114
Georgia	36.1	63.9	70	194
Virginia	34.6	65.4	27	78
North Carolina	25.7	74.3	43	167
South Carolina	18.5	81.5	40	216
Texas	12.3	87.7	29	236
Arkansas	4.8	95.2	13	272

Table 7.2 *Reported Destinations of Migrants after Reconstruction—Selected States*

State	Percentage of Migrants	Number of Migrants
Arkansas	53.9	330
Texas	10.3	63
Oklahoma	7.4	45
Indiana	5.1	31
Florida	4.0	25
Ohio	3.3	20
Missouri	3.3	20
Total	87.3	534

able that the women had very little choice in their work. More than two-thirds were servants—nurses and maids, laundresses, and cooks—and most of the remainder had worked on a farm. Desirable jobs were practically impossible for them to obtain.

These continuing patterns of economic and racial exploitation testified to the survival of a social system, not merely a few isolated elements of it. Although the South was beginning to industrialize, it remained a predominantly agricultural region controlled by a wealthy elite of planters' families. Their control of the best land preserved their economic power while they branched out into new areas of enterprise. Politically and socially they dominated the blacks and poor whites by setting these two groups against each other. Subjection of the Negro, the talisman of race, was the central element of a social ideology that buttressed and extended the elite's power.[7] Racism in slightly new forms performed the same function for the social system that slavery had once served, and racial oppression was essential to the ends of the system. Thus, little had changed for the black man, either practically or theoretically.

[164]

Table 7.3   *Reported Occupations in Freedom—Males*

Occupations	Percentage	Number
Agriculture	48.6	362
Personal service	8.1	60
Industry	24.1	179
Skilled workers	6.5	48
White collar	8.7	65
Business	2.2	14
Other	1.9	14
Total	100.1	744

Table 7.4   *Reported Occupations in Freedom —Females*

Occupations	Percentage	Number
Agriculture	19.0	89
Personal service	66.9	313
Industry ·	1.1	5
Skilled workers	6.6	31
White collar	2.6	12
Business	0.8	4
Other	3.0	14
Total	100.0	468

Since social conditions had changed so little, it was natural that many forms of black accommodation and resistance remained the same. To stress the difference between white status and black status, planters and other whites continued to demand extreme deference from Negroes, and Negroes continued to give it. Here, skills at role playing and dissimulation remained useful. Blacks could adjust their actions to appease angry dirt farmers or charm wealthy landowners who still displayed a paternalistic style. The threat of leaving to seek employment elsewhere became a lever to pry better conditions from the landowner, in ways similar to the effect of hiding in the woods under slavery. To affirm and strengthen their mental resistance, meetings of blacks away from white supervision remained vital.

The forms of a separate black social life multiplied greatly after the war, because distance from the master in private affairs had been one of the chief gains of freedom. Families moved away from the master to live by themselves. Black churches now stood in the open whereas worship formerly had to be in secret. Stolen hours of communication within the slave quarters gave way to an expanded community life in all-black settlements and towns. Each of these activities, now strengthened, developed a sense of separate identity and unity among the former slaves and set them further apart from the whites. It may well have been that Reconstruction and the era of segregation that followed it imparted greater impetus to black culture than slavery had in its last decades. Bondage had helped create a separate mentality, but bondage interfered with the expression of black unity. During and after Reconstruction the former slaves had much greater opportunity to come together and share common values and beliefs away from white supervision. The freedmen's aim during Reconstruction had not been to mix with whites but, as one man put it, "to be darkies amongst ourselves."[8] In this more favorable setting the black culture could elaborate itself and develop greater unity and strength. Thus, freedom accentuated black identity and permitted the consummation of cultural desires that had been partially blocked in slavery.

Another form of resistance that remained very pervasive after the war was theft. Denied the fruits of their labor, as they had been in slavery, blacks continued to appropriate goods. "We were so hongry we were bound to steal or parish," said Louisa

Adams, who went on to observe that "this trait seems to be handed down from slavery days." The fact that some masters had encouraged their slaves to steal from other planters reinforced the practice. Herdsmen complained loudly throughout the South that freedmen were stealing and butchering their cattle and hogs, and this agitation led to the well-known pig laws that put many blacks in jail. Nevertheless, theft continued as a covert means of redressing systematic exploitation.[9]

Direct responses to injustice, such as political action, had become hopeless shortly after the end of Reconstruction, and the former slaves who were interviewed expressed nearly universal and total disillusionment with politics. Sneed Teague delivered a typical comment when he asserted, "I don't care nothin' bout votin'." Like him, most blacks had long since ceased to "enquire . . . bout politics." No political movement excited their interest until the New Deal offered hope of relief and old-age pensions. With a depth of gratitude that was both revealing and touching, many informants praised Franklin Delano Roosevelt for recognizing their plight and including them in programs to help the poor. "Thank God, Mr. Roosevelt come 'long," said one man. "Him never ask whether us democrat or 'publican nor was us black or white; him just clothe our nakedness and ease de pains of hunger. . . . Oh, how I love dat man." Extending the religious imagery with which many discussed Roosevelt, Reuben Rosborough said that Lincoln had been "raised up by de Lord, just like Moses, to free a 'culiar people. I think Mr. Roosevelt is de Joshua dat come after him. . . . God bless him and 'stain him in his. . .work to bring de kingdom of heaven into and upon de earth."[10]

Reuben Rosborough's faith that God ruled over all and was moving to bring His kingdom to the earth typified the religious convictions of nearly all the former slaves. From specific events, the tone of their interviews, and their whole demeanor, it was obvious that the former slaves were a God-centered people. Religious faith had provided one of the supporting pillars of their existence. Through long lives of trouble and disappointment, they had clung to their faith in God, and they continued to believe that God would bring justice in heaven and on earth.

As they discussed their lives, more than half of the former slaves found opportunities to interject their views on the importance of religion, even when no questions on the subject were asked. Only a small handful denied that religion was important to them, and probably the great majority had an active faith in God. Many agreed with Eugenia Fair, who thought that "everybody ought to join a church." Several testified that the church's influence had helped them to "live better" and to "do better for their families." Religion organized life for many black communities and individuals and gave it a higher purpose.[11]

The faith of the former slaves could produce a galvanizing effect on even the most elderly churchgoers. "I still shouts at meetin's," admitted Ellen Payne, who explained that she had no control over movements of the spirit: "It hits me jes' like a streak of lightning, and there ain't no holdin' it." Deep emotional fervor had always distinguished black religion from the services of middle- and upper-class whites. The former slaves were aware of this difference and believed that they gave themselves to God more fully and truly. Noting that whites came to her church to hear the singing, Dinah Cunningham suggested that perhaps blacks sang better because "us does love de Lord just a little bit better, and what's in our mouth is in our hearts." The faith of the whites had not produced good works; therefore, blacks felt that it must be shallow and dead. When another woman employed superlatives to describe the moral character of her former master, the highest praise she could give him was to distinguish him from other whites and say that he sought religion "same as any colored person."[12]

One function of black Christianity had been to provide consolation through the long and bitterly disappointing years. Manda Walker said, for example, that she had "a instinct dat God'll make it all right over and up yonder and dat all our 'flic-tions will, in de long run, turn out to our 'ternal welfare and happiness." But this was not the sole effect of religion on the blacks, for their God had always been a god of justice who punished transgressors for their misdeeds. Thus, the black faith nourished a passion for social justice and expressed the blacks' bitter opposition to the whites, who one day would have to pay. "These people can't beat up us people and jump up on a bed and close their eyes and die and expect to go to heaven," said one man who believed in justice and resistance as well as heavenly rewards. [13]

Beyond religion another institution had helped the former slaves endure and overcome life's trials—the family. Although the narratives' informants did not boast about their family life, they provided information that testified to an impressive degree of family stability. As one reads through the slave narratives, one commonly encounters married couples who had been together forty, fifty, sixty, or even more years. Among three hundred twenty-eight former slaves who provided information on the length of their longest marriage, the average length of marriage was forty-four and one-half years and the median was more than forty-nine years. Even more impressive data from a much larger group of former slaves revealed the widespread strength of marriages and the infrequency of divorce and desertion as causes of separation. A large majority of the former slaves who supplied information had been married only once, as table 7.5 indicates. Since many of the individuals interviewed had already lived into their late seventies or eighties, it was not surprising that many of them had married a second time after being widowed. Almost 90 percent of the former slaves had been married only once or twice, and fewer than 9 percent reported three, four, or more marriages. Rarely did broken marriages result from incompatibility of the partners or the irresponsibility, immorality, or desertion of a spouse. As table 7.6 shows, the predominant cause of separation was death.

The narratives contain other valuable information on the

Table 7.5   Number of Marriages Reported by Former Slaves

Number of Marriages	Percentage	Number
None	2.8	34
One	68.7	842
Two	20.1	246
Three	5.1	62
Four	2.0	24
More than four	1.5	18
Total	100.2	1226

Table 7.6   Reasons for Separation of Marriage Partners

	Percentage			
Reason	First Marriage (N = 780)	Second Marriage (N = 242)	Third Marriage (N = 66)	Fourth Marriage (N = 25)
No separation	17.8	31.4	34.8	16.0
Death	71.9	54.1	50.0	60.0
Decision to divorce	6.4	10.3	10.6	12.0
Desertion	3.3	3.7	3.0	8.0
Other	0.4	0.4	1.5	4.0

characteristics of black families. Herbert Gutman argued in *The Black Family in Slavery and Freedom* that an important feature of black social patterns was the tendency for men to be considerably older than their wives. The evidence of the narratives supports this finding. Men married, on the average, at the age of 27.6, whereas women first married at 19.5. The median age at marriage for males was 24.9; for females it was 18.4. As a rural folk, blacks tended to select their mates from the areas adjacent to their own farm or district and, like other groups of farmers, usually had large families. The average number of children was 8.5.

The former slaves typically had to work far into old age before they could find rest and retirement. Low-paying jobs and discrimination gave them few chances to save money, and most had to depend upon themselves as long as possible. The average age at retirement for the former slaves was a staggering 80.7 years, which demonstrated that few benefited much from the oft-mentioned charity of white southerners toward their faithful black retainers. After aged men and women could work no longer, they turned to their children and other relatives for support. As table 7.7 shows, the family and various branches of government supplied the lion's share of aid for elderly blacks who had passed their productive years. White charity reached relatively few, while nearly one-fifth of the former slaves, especially the women, reported that they lived with their children or other relatives.

People in this kind of economic situation had to do what was necessary to survive, and throughout most of the former slaves' lives what was necessary had meant accommodating themselves to the whites and mollifying them to avoid trouble

Table 7.7   Primary Source of Aid at Time of Interview

Source of Aid	Percentage	Number
Family	48.5	424
Government	38.1	333
Other blacks	3.4	30
White charity	8.4	73
Other	1.5	13
Total	99.9	873

or gain some benefit. These survival skills had proved essential in slavery. Through later years the former slaves had perfected them and still employed them at the time of the interviews, a fact that can cause confusion for the careless reader. The narratives are full of accommodating statements that say much more about the informant's social circumstances than about his personal views on race relations. For example, one man who manifested faith in the "better class" of whites had been a school teacher and, therefore, had been compelled to satisfy the white power structure as a condition of continuing his work. Another woman, who had been fortunate enough to work for wealthy white families, protected her interests (and bragged about her success) by stressing that she got along well with whites and "ain't never been much of a hand to run 'round wid colored folks."[14]

As they neared the end of their lives, however, even some of the most ingratiating former slaves tended to become more demanding and to reveal that their humility was an investment from which they expected a return. In a petitioning vein, Ed Barber reminded his interviewer that he had supported South Carolina's Redeemers and then said, "I begs you, in de name of . . . Wade Hampton, not to forget me in dis old age pension business." Ann Hawthorne was more demanding. She had just become disabled when the depression struck; consequently, she decided that she had to do something. "I git on my walkin' stick," she remembered, "and I wag up town and I didn' fail to ax de white folks 'cause I wo' myself out wukkin' for 'em." Upon learning that the interviewer was receiving pay, another woman quickly asked, "What is you gwine to give me?"[15]

After years of accommodation, blacks could demand aid from their white employers, and some made it clear that they played the role of loyal retainer because it was the only way to survive. John Hamilton explained that he depended on the whites to help him because "dese pore colored folks ain't got nuttin'." Two women who made extremely accomodationist statements also revealed that they drew close to whites for practical advantages, not out of affection. Maggie Perkins said, "I tells the young fry to give honor to the white folks, and my preacher tell 'em to obey the white folks, dat dey are our best friends, dey is our dependence and it would be hard getting on if we didn't have em to help us." Another woman revealed the same search for benefits that lay behind accommodation: "My mother always said, 'Tillie, always tie to the bes' white folks. Them that has inflooence, 'cause if you gits into trouble they can git you out.' "16

Because so many of the former slaves had had to live their lives by such rules, they often felt a little uncomfortable about the rising generation of young, more assertive blacks. Complaints that the new generation "ain't bein' raised like we was" and didn't "have no manners" frequently appeared. Henry Smith probably spoke truly when he said, "The old race can get along a lot better with the white folks than the young race can."17 Younger blacks were maturing and bringing heightened aspirations into a world that was becoming bigger and less rural, with less face-to-face contact between blacks and whites. The young blacks did not share the same perceptions of what might be possible for them. Their lack of caution disturbed their elders and aroused ingrained reflexes of fear.

Yet another part of the former slaves' dissatisfaction with the young stemmed from eager hopes that the next generation would make great progress and enjoy a better life. With the impatience of those who have forgotten what it is like to be young and enjoying oneself, some of the former slaves wanted to see more evidence that black youths were working hard and saving money. "Dey am too wild," lamented Campbell Davis, who wanted young people to study so that they "could make something out [of] deyselves." Cigarettes, whiskey, and too much partying would not bring progress, some informants feared. But a few were both more tolerant and more hopeful about the new habits of the young. Allen Manning argued that it was precisely because the young Negroes were unfamiliar with old ways of thinking that "lots of them are rising up and amounting to something. . . . You see, it's because they been taught that they got as good a show to be something as anybody, if they tries hard." Simp Campbell believed that "the young race of our people is progressin' fine" and would use whatever opportunities might result from a relaxation of the color line.[18]

When pressed by white interviewers, many of the former slaves admitted that in their lives slavery had carried certain advantages. "I had it better den dan I does now," said Caroline Farrow, who stressed the importance of having "plenty to eat." "Us have warm clothes and plenty to eat and de dry place to live," agreed James Boyd; he added, "Dat more'n lots of niggers has now." One of those who was suffering during the depression remarked bluntly, "It hard to be hongry and dat I's been many times lately." As a result of this hardship, Aaron Russel stated, "Times lately I's wish I's back with de massa, 'cause I has plenty rations dere."[19]

Statements such as these occurred frequently; yet many of the former slaves took pains to ensure that whites did not misinterpret their feelings. One man, who declared that he had been more contented as a slave and had done less "frettin'," quickly added, "Course, I don' want to go back into slavery." Another informant stressed that she longed for the superior material conditions, not the state of slavery itself. When told that one former slave had declared a preference for slavery, Thomas Johns reacted defiantly. "Anybody which says that is tellin a lie," he retorted. "Dere is sumpin 'bout bein' free and dat makes up for all de hardships. I'se been both slave and free and I knows." Others who frankly acknowledged that poverty and worry had plagued their lives since emancipation still insisted that "being free de best time to lib." "I think slavery was wrong," one man asserted forthrightly. "[I] don't think one man ought to own another man." William McWhorter politely but bluntly told an obtuse white interviewer, "Now, Mistess, you knows all

Niggers would ruther be free, and I ain't no diffunt from nobody else 'bout dat. . . . Dat Jeff Davis ought to be 'shamed of hisself to want Niggers kept in bondage . . . you can't 'spect us Niggers to b'lieve he was so awful good."[20]

As they came to the close of their lives, the former slaves manifested substantial pride in their race. Parents had taught their children to reject the prejudiced images of blacks that white people sought to impose. "I had always been told from the time I was a small child," recalled one woman, "that I was a Negro of African stock. That it was no disgrace to be a Negro." Others spoke of the achievements of blacks in America. "The cullud folks has been here more'n a hunerd years," said one man, "and has help make the United States what it is." This pride in their race led a few to voice explicit commitments to black nationalism while others expressed faith that conditions in America would improve in the future. "De Lord not gwine to hold His hand any longer 'ginst us," prophesized Anne Broome. "Us cleared de forests, built de railroads, cleaned up de swamps, and nursed de white folks." Perhaps Pierce Harper summed up the former slaves' feelings most simply and eloquently in words that could stand as the testament for his generation: "I been always trying to help my people to rise 'bove their station and they are rising all the time, and some day they'll be free."[21]

Reproduced from the collection of the Library of Congress

Afterword

What do the slave narratives reveal about slavery? How do they alter and inform our understanding of the peculiar institution that had such a great impact on the development of the United States?

Through countless books and articles historians have wrestled with this topic. Its central place in the American story has brooded over their work, tinged their thinking with regional or racial loyalties, and influenced their interpretations with concern for political realities, past and future. Probably no subject in American history has been more frequently researched; yet dominant interpretations have shifted rapidly in rough relationship to the transformations of contemporary race relations. To be sure, each age must write its own history and rediscover a usable past, but if a scholarly discipline is to demonstrate its integrity, it should fix some landmarks in the midst of an ever-changing scene.

Instead, conclusions on basic issues such as the importance of race versus class, the degree of difference between white and black cultures, and the severity and effects of slavery have changed frequently. When racism pervaded all parts of the nation, scholars did not hesitate to label the slave population as culturally different from the white. Of course, such interpretations stressed the inferiority or savagery of the blacks. It was ironic, however, that a commitment to civil rights led historians to forget black culture in the rush to assert that blacks and whites were the same and, therefore, equal. Similarly, when prejudice was overt and explicit, some historians proudly defended the racism that animated slavery, whereas improvements in the racial climate have encouraged recent work that minimizes race in favor of class. And though apologists for the South once complacently underestimated the damage done by slavery, some modern supporters of social justice have greatly exaggerated the horrors of bondage.

To some extent the explanation for these oscillations is conventional and unsurprising; for no historian can escape his environment, and individuals will always pursue different perspectives in the search for knowledge. Yet, beneath these influences, I think, lie some deeper causes that have produced this historians' dilemma. The chameleonlike alterations of interpretation reveal both a deeply ingrained tendency within the dominant white culture and a persistent defect of historical methodology.

Throughout our history white Americans have assumed that they knew what was best for blacks and the nation. They argued that the race problem was their problem—theirs to define, analyze, and resolve. Liberals of the 1960s, for example, typically believed that they knew what Negroes wanted and that all would be well if black people were given access to the benefits of white society. Few considered the possibility that blacks might desire a different solution or that they might disapprove both of their exclusion from the mainstream of society and of the nature and goals of that society itself.

This thinking was symptomatic of a provincial mentality. Although we live in a multiracial world, few Americans have gained a multiracial consciousness. Accordingly, a history that recognizes the perspectives and impact of all groups has been slow to develop. Many histories of the United States are actually only histories of white Americans or of what white people have done to Negroes. As long as whites conceive the past and future in terms of their own group alone, they will alter and revise the written record to conform to changing images of themselves. Thus, the history of blacks has been shaped to express whites' perceptions of themselves. As the political environment has changed, historians have recast the record of white cruelty or compassion, justice or injustice.

Partly as a result of this mentality, most historians have restricted themselves to white sources. Records that give the perspective of the slaves are relatively scarce and unconventional in form, but scholars have shown a disposition not to use them in any event. Yet, these sources are essential if one is to understand a biracial reality. To know the true character of slavery, one must know what blacks thought about it, how they felt about it, and how they regarded the whites who fomented it. Too many factors—prejudice, self-interest, defensiveness about outside critics, even wishful thinking—clouded the whites' perceptions of the slaves to take only their word on a two-sided relationship.

The slave narratives provide a window on the thoughts and feelings of those in bondage. The view from this window may not be perfect, and it may be more difficult to see into some areas than others, but the rewards are well worth the effort. Through the narratives we can locate some fixed points on the complicated terrain of slavery.

What landmarks do the narratives give us? They make clear, first of all, that masters did not control the minds of their bondsmen. Most slaves were uneducated and had little experience of the world beyond their county, but their minds had not turned as a result into malleable clay, which the master could shape to his liking. The slaves retained their self-respect and sense of justice and hated the master for his cruelty toward them. They were not pitiful infants but angry men and women who had to endure unfavorable conditions that were not in their power to change.

Clearly also religion played a major role in protecting the dignity and self-esteem that were vital to America's bondsmen. The frequency of their professions of faith and the depth of their devotion should place this fact beyond question. Their preference for separate worship and their views on theft also indicate that they were not trapped by the whites' self-serving definitions of ethics. Armed with a belief in God's justice and goodness, the slaves could endure what they had to endure without surrendering their sense of worth or resentment of mistreatment.

Another force that strengthened the slaves was their separate and distinct Afro-American culture. Too much had happened for them to be able to preserve Africa in the United States, but they became Afro-Americans, not merely Americans. African music, art, dance, and language patterns and the non-European power over nature associated with conjuring and voodoo gave them a special identity as a people and bound their group closer together.

An essential part of this cohesion derived from race and the slaves' awareness of themselves as a despised racial group. The former slaves remind us that they were oppressed because their skins were black, and historians should not deemphasize the fact that racism was a basic part of antebellum American slavery. Racial oppression produced racial consciousness; the slaves carried with them out of slavery a fundamental suspicion of white people. In this sense America has always been two nations, for the black community retains today a sense of closeness among its members that is the other half of a sense of distance from whites.

The ability of the slaves to defend their humanity under pressure does not suggest that slavery was less than cruel. But it does remind us that the cruelty of bondage consisted of the denial of physical comforts and rewards, the pain of beatings and overwork, and the anguish of subjection to another rather than of mental debasement or destruction. America's slaves were abused physically, exploited economically, separated at times from their loved ones, denied education and opportunity, and deprived of freedom. Many slaves had to endure lives as beasts of burden, but they did not lose their mental independence.

It may seem surprising that bondage's impact was not

worse. The former slaves' ability to survive such mistreatment and emerge whole suggests a toughness and resiliency about human nature that this author had not fully expected. But one of the strongest traits of human beings is their ability to adapt and adjust to circumstances. The testimony of the former slaves proves that if men have a body of culture on which to rely, they can endure conditions that are very unfavorable indeed. The narratives give little evidence of group pathologies produced by frustration, but they do provide abundant evidence of persistent and continuing group resistance. That the slaves were not crushed and achieved as much as they did is a tribute to them as well as a source of encouragement to all who ponder man's future in a troubled world.

Appendix A
Methods of Recording
and Coding Information

One of the goals of this book has been to present a systematic, not merely impressionistic, analysis of the slave narratives. Because computers have enormous capacities for storing and retrieving information, a computer was used in this study. The mathematical and statistical techniques employed were elementary, but the reader should know something about the manner in which information was classified, recorded, and fed into the computer for analysis.

After examination of a sample drawn from the collections of narratives, the author chose eighty-one variables, or categories of information, for the computerized portion of the study. These variables included

the state in which the interview took place
the race of the interviewer
the sex of the interviewer
a unique number assigned to each interviewer
the year of birth of the former slave
the sex of the former slave
the race of the former slave's father
the race of the former slave's mother
the race of the former slave's grandparents
the occupation of the former slave's father
the occupation of the former slave's mother
where the former slave's parents lived (same plantation, different
    plantations, etc.)

the number of children in that family
the primary state in which the former slave resided during slavery
the primary state in which the former slave resided during
    Reconstruction
the size of the plantation on which the former slave lived during slavery
the sex of the master
the principal crop grown on the plantation
the occupation of the former slave in slavery
the marital status of the former slave during slavery
whether the family unit to which the former slave belonged during
    slavery was broken by slavery
the former slave's rating of his food during slavery
the former slave's reports on cruel treatment that he received in
    bondage
the former slave's reports on cruel treatment of others on the plantation
the perpetrator of the cruelty
acts of resistance committed by the former slave while in bondage
another state code (for a file on other slaves' resistance)
acts of resistance by other slaves
the age of the resister
the sex of the resister
the marital status of the resister
the occupation of the resister
the cause of the resistance
the size of the plantation on which the resistance occurred
conditions on that plantation
the money possessed by the former slave during bondage
the source of the money possessed by the former slave
the former slave's attitude toward the master
actions by the master at the end of the Civil War
the former slave's experiences with United States troops
whether the former slave stayed with the master or left after freedom
whether other slaves stayed with the master or left after freedom
the former slave's reasons for staying or leaving
the other slaves' reasons for staying or leaving
where those who left went
the number of moves by the former slave
whether women worked in the fields after slavery
the former slave's choice of name, its origin
the former slave's occupation in freedom
the terms of agricultural labor for the former slave during
    Reconstruction

the farmer's share in sharecropping
political activity engaged in by the former slave
educational attainments of the former slave
the former slave's experiences with the Ku Klux Klan
reports on other freedmen's experiences with the Klan
the Klan's purpose
the former slave's attitude toward religion
the amount of continued contact by the freedman with whites
the number of marriages for the former slave
the age at first marriage for the former slave
the duration of the former slave's longest marriage
the number of children born to the former slave
the race of the former slave's mate
the occupation of the former slave's mate
the location of the former slave's mate at time of marriage
reasons for separation of any of the former slave's marriages (six
    maximum)
the former slave's age at retirement
the former slave's estimated age at retirement, if exact age is
    unobtainable
the amount of land owned by the former slave
whether the former slave lived with relatives at the time of the
    interview
the number of people in that household
sources of outside aid for the former slave
institutions to which the former slave belonged
whether the former slave believed in haunts
whether the former slave believed in conjuration and superstitions
whether the former slave had knowledge of root medicines.

Using a form that listed each of these categories of information, the author then read each narrative carefully and recorded whatever information was available (while also taking conventional notes). No narrative contained data for every one of these variables, and a few narratives mentioned only ten or twelve of the areas under examination. After this information was punched onto cards, however, the computer could use it to summarize the information from 2358 narratives for one variable, compare two variables with each other, or select a particular group of narratives according to some characteristic and examine that group further. In comparisons (or cross tabulations) of one variable with another, only narratives that contained information on both variables would be used. These capabilities of the computer made possible the tables that appear in the text.

In recording and coding the information, decisions had to be made. At times these decisions were easy and at times difficult. Sometimes decisions could be based upon objective criteria, but sometimes a degree of subjectivity was inescapable. The former slave's year of birth, for example, might appear in the narrative, or the reader might have to ferret it out by deduction from clues that existed; it was even possible that the former slave might state a year of birth that was plainly erroneous. Identifying a reliable year for the former slave's birth, however, was not too difficult. An example of a more challenging area would be the coding of the former slaves' statements about whether they left their plantation after the Civil War. Often narratives contained statements such as "We left right away," "Soon my daddy came and got us," or "After awhile we left." To deal with the lack of specificity in this information, the author selected categories that made the decisions on coding less difficult: left during the war, left within a week after freedom, left in one month, left later than one month but earlier than one year, etc.

The most difficult decisions on coding were those that involved the former slaves' attitudes, for the whole atmosphere of the interview had to be taken into account and explicit statements might not sum up the former slave's views. How frankly, for example, could a black person reveal his feelings to a white person in the segregated South of the 1930s? The former slaves often contradicted themselves during their interviews, first praising the memory of their old master and those happy days and only later mentioning inhumanities that had affected them or their loved ones. Like many others, Callie Elder in the Georgia narratives found an opportunity early in her story to say that her owners "was jus' as good to us as dey could be." Such praise seemed to be almost a ritual required by the social situation. Less than a page later, this same Callie Elder was describing the whippings on the plantation and lamenting that her father and grandfather suffered under the lash with great frequency. Other former slaves echoed the words, "They were just as good as they could be," and then went on to tell of their mothers being sold away from them or of their fathers fleeing to escape a beating. If specific incidents within the body of the narrative contradicted a positive statement made at the beginning, this author placed greater weight on the incident itself and the way in which it was described. If strong positive statements about the master went uncontradicted throughout the narrative, the author coded the former slave's attitude as "very favorable." On the whole, the author doubts that other researchers would reach completely different results. Naturally some variations would appear over 2358 cases, but the general picture would probably remain the same. Further information on coding will be made available to anyone who requests it.

Appendix B
Race of Interviewers

In the case of some individuals, the typescript of the narratives identifies their race. For the rest, the identifications given here were based on textual evidence, such as forms of address or reference to the interviewer's race by the informant.

South Carolina
Whites:
  Caldwell Sims
  Henry Grant
  F. S. DuPre
  W. W. Dixon
  Annie Ruth Davis
  Genevieve W. Chandler
  Jessie A. Butler
  Phoebe Faucette
  H. Grady Davis
  Stiles M. Scruggs
  C. S. Murray

Blacks:
  Augustus Ladson

Race Unidentified:
  Everett R. Pierce
  G. Leland Summer
  Martha S. Pinckney
  Cassels R. Tiedeman
  Mrs. Lucile Young
  Hattie Mobley

Gyland H. Hamlin
Chlotilde R. Martin
Ellie S. Rice
Samuel Addison
Laura L. Middleton

Texas
Race Unidentified:
  Fred Dibble
  Rheba Beehler

Alabama
Whites:
  Mary A. Poole
  Susie R. O'Brien
  Gertha Couric
  Ila Prine
  John Morgan Smith
  Ruby Pickens
  W. F. Jordan
  Alexander B. Johnson
  Mrs. Preston Klein
  Demps Oden

Margaret Fowler
Annie D. Dean
Francois Ludgere Diard
Alice L. Barton
Woodrow Hand
Daphne L. E. Curtis
Proctor Mills
William B. Strickland
David Holt

Blacks:
Levi D. Shelby, Jr.

Race Unidentified:
Ira S. Jordan
Petterson Marzoni
Mabel Farrior
Lois Lynn
Edward F. Harper
Jack Kytle
G. L. Clark
A. B. Johnson
J. R. Jones
Mildred Scott Taylor

Indiana
Whites:
Iris Cook
Henrietta Karwowski

Blacks:
Harry Jackson

Race Unidentified:
Lauana Creel
Emery Turner
William Webb Tuttle
Anna Pritchett
Robert C. Irvin
Wm. R. Mays
Walter R. Harris
Grace Monroe
Albert Strope
Archie Koritz

Cecil C. Miller
Virginia Tully
Estella R. Dodson
Beulah Van Meter
Emily Hobson

Oklahoma
None Identified

Mississippi
Whites:
Mrs. Richard Kolb
Edith Wyatt Moore
Mrs. Carrie Campbell
Mrs. C. E. Wills
W. B. Allison

Race Unidentified:
Esther de Sola
Mrs. W. F. Holmes
Marjorie Woods Austin

Arkansas
Whites:
Irene Robertson
Watt McKinney
Mrs. Zillah Cross Peel
Mrs. Bernice Bowden
Mary D. Hudgins
Rosa B. Ingram
Beulah Sherwood Hagg
Thomas Elmore Lucy
Mrs. Annie L. LaCotts
Mrs. Mildred Thompson
Mrs. Carol Graham
Cecil Copeland
Mrs. Blanche Edwards

Blacks:
Samuel S. Taylor
Pernella Anderson
Sallie C. Miller

Race Unidentified:
R. S. Taylor
Velma Sample
Mrs. W. M. Ball
Martin and Barker
Miss Hazel Horn

Missouri
Whites:
Mollie E. Smith
Bernard Hinkle
Dovie Rose

Blacks:
Grace E. White

Race Unidentified:
J. Tom Miles
Carl B. Boyer
Kathleen Williams

Georgia
Whites:
Sadie B. Hornsby
Henrietta Carlisle
Elizabeth Watson
Grace McCune
Minnie Branham Stonestreet
Sarah H. Hall
Geneva Tonsill
Leila Harris
Joseph E. Jaffee
Mrs. Margaret Johnson
Louise Oliphant
Alberta Minor
Ruth Chitty
Mary Crawford
Velma Bell
Louise McKinney
Emily Powell
Estelle G. Burke
Annie Lee Newton
John N. Booth
Ruth H. Sanford

Blacks:
Minnie B. Ross
E. Driskell
Adella S. Dixon
Josephine Lowell

Race Unidentified:
J. R. Jones
Maude Barragan
Corry Fowler
Mrs. Mattie B. Roberts
Willie H. Cole

North Carolina
Whites:
T. Pat Matthews
Travis Jordan
Mary A. Hicks
Mrs. Edith S. Hibbs
Marjorie Jones
Esther S. Pinnix
Miss Nancy Woodburn Watkins
Daisey Whaley
Mrs. W. N. Harriss

Kansas
Whites:
Leta Gray

Race Unidentified:
E. Jean Foote

Kentucky
Whites:
Eliza Ison
Kenneth Jones
L. Cherry
Cecelia Laswell
Perry Larkey
John Forsee
Mamie Hanberry

Race Unidentified:
Hazel Cinnamon

Mildred Roberts
Ruby Garten
Carl F. Hall
Gertrude Vogler
Byers York
Pearl House
Margaret Bishop
Evelyn McLemore

Maryland
Whites:
_____ Guthrie
Ellen B. Warfield
_____ Stansbury

Blacks:
_____ Rogers

Ohio
Whites:
Frank M. Smith
James Immel
Hallie Miller
Miriam Logan
George Conn
Sarah Probst

Race Unidentified:
Ruth Thompson
Chas. McCullough
Albert I. Dugin
K. Osthimer
Betty Lugabill
_____ Bishop
Rev. Edward Knox
Forest H. Lees

Tennessee
Whites:
Della Yoe

Florida
Whites:
Jules A. Frost

Blacks:
Rachel A. Austin
Martin Richardson
Pearl Randolph
Alfred Farrell
James Johnson
Viola B. Muse
Samuel Johnson
L. Rebecca Baker

Race Unidentified:
Cora M. Taylor
Barbara Darsey

Virginia★
Whites:
Sue K. Gordon
Lucille B. Jayne
Margaret Jeffries
Bernice Lewis
Essie W. Smith
Mary S. Venable
I. M. Warren

Blacks:
Claude W. Anderson
Susie R. C. Byrd
Thelma Dunston
Frances V. Green
David Hoggard
William T. Lee
George E. Majette
Faith Morris
Milton L. Randolph
Marietta Silver
Isaiah Volley
Jessie R. Williams
Emmy Wilson

★Taken from Charles L. Perdue, Jr., Thomas E. Barden, and Robert K. Phillips, eds., *Weevils in the Wheat.*

Appendix C
Additional Tables

Table C.1 Responses Obtained by White and Black Interviewers—Selected Areas of Difference

Race of Interviewer	Percentage						
	Father Was White	Born before 1851	Were Field Hands in Slavery	Were Whipped	Reported Forced Sex on Plantation	Left to Avoid Master	Believed in Haunts, Etc.
White	4.7	26.5	18.8	59.4	6.8	14.7	79.1
Black	10.1	40.6	26.0	69.7	14.4	23.5	87.5

Table C.2 Responses Obtained by Different Interviewers—Selected Areas of Difference

Race and Sex of Interviewer	Percentage					
	Father Was White	Rated Food as Good	Were Whipped	Reported Forced Sex on Plantation	Were Very Unfavorable toward Master	Reported Master Gave Material Aid at End of War
White male	5.3	62.7	39.3	8.6	9.2	36.8
White female	4.4	76.3	64.4	6.1	5.6	22.6
Black male	7.6	44.4	75.0	13.1	17.4	16.7
Black female	13.3	50.8	64.7	18.0	21.4	27.0

Table C.3   Sex of Interviewers

Sex	Percentage	Number
Male	26.9	635
Female	48.2	1136
Both sexes present	1.9	45
Not determined	23.0	542
Total	100.0	2358

Table C.4   Sex of Former Slaves

Sex	Percentage	Number
Male	49.8	1175
Female	49.9	1176
Not determined	0.3	7
Total	100.0	2358

Table C.5   Age of Slaves and Attitude toward Master (N = 1485)

	Percentage		
Attitude	*Born Before 1851 (N = 582)*	*Born 1851–1860 (N = 766)*	*Born After 1860 (N = 137)*
Very favorable	7.7	10.3	5.1
Favorable	56.2	61.4	67.9
Unfavorable	21.5	19.6	18.2
Very unfavorable	13.7	7.3	8.8
Ambivalent	0.9	1.4	0.0

Appendix D
New Narratives

After this book was written, Greenwood Press published Supplement, Series I to *The American Slave: A Composite Autobiography*. This supplement made available twelve volumes of additional slave narratives, both totally new accounts and previously undiscovered versions of older interviews. To obtain these documents, George P. Rawick and his co-workers, including Jan Hillegas, Ken Lawrence, and Norman Yetman, combed through the holdings of archives and libraries in several states. Due to their efforts our record of the Federal Writers' Project's work on slavery is nearly complete. Scholars stand in debt to these individuals, who may publish still more narratives in the future.

How do these new narratives affect the findings of this book? Do they present a significantly different picture of slavery, or do they merely build upon and expand the information given here? Although George Rawick admitted that some of these accounts were inferior in quality to the original collection of narratives, he also suggested that they might contain some valuable new material. For example, the geographical coverage of these new materials was wider. Moreover, some Mississippi narratives, Rawick felt, might have been suppressed because they were too critical of slaveholders.

To investigate these questions, the author examined a random sample drawn from the approximately 1070 totally new narratives and read each of the approximately 68 narratives for which an earlier version exists. For each new group of narratives information was collected in the categories described in Appendix A, and the results were then tabulated and compared with information found in the originally published collection. Tables D.1 through D.5 present some of the information gleaned from the random sample of new documents. In each table the size of the random sample is one hundred.

A moment's inspection will show that these tables are virtually identical to tables I.3, I.4, I.7, 7.5, and 7.6 presented in the text. In these important areas of slave experience and attitudes there was no significant difference between the sample of totally new narratives and the original collection. Both this quantitative test and impressionistic evidence indicate that these new narratives would not produce a drastic revision of the findings of this study, though the supplementary information they contain is valuable. In one respect the Mississippi narratives proved disappointing, for a large portion of them consisted of short and rather superficial accounts constructed from newspaper stories about former slaves.

Tables D.6 and D.7 summarize the extent to which information in the new versions of older accounts agreed with or differed from the originals. Here again, there is relatively little disagreement between information in the new versions of narratives and the original versions. The newly published documents expand our knowledge but do not drastically alter it. Perhaps the care taken in reading each narrative, as described at the end of Appendix A, served as a safeguard against gross misrepresentation of the slaves' point of view. In any case the author feels that a complete analysis of the additional slave narratives would yield results quite similar to those presented in this study.

Table D.1   *Attitude toward Master (N = 43)*

Attitude toward Master

Very favorable	2.0
Favorable	65.0
Unfavorable	23.0
Very unfavorable	9.0

Table D.2   *Decision to Stay with or Leave Master at End of War (N = 49)*

Decision	Percentage
Left during war	4.0
Left immediately	2.0
Left within one year	28.0
Left, time uncertain	10.0
Stayed one to five years	10.0
Stayed several years or more	35.0
Stayed, time uncertain	8.0
Left but returned	2.0

Table D.3   *Occupations in Slavery of Those Interviewed (N = 52)*

Occupation	Percentage
House servants	29.0
Field hands	27.0
Artisans	2.0
None or child's chores	42.0

Table D.4   Number of Marriages Reported by Former Slaves (N = 44)

Number of Marriages	Percentage
None	2.0
One	64.0
Two	20.0
Three	11.0
Four	0.0
More than four	2.0

Table D.5   Reasons for Separation of Marriage Partners (First Marriage) (N = 26)

Reason	Percentage
No separation	23.0
Death	65.0
Divorce	4.0
Desertion	8.0

Table D.6   Treatment of Key Issues

Issue	New Narrative Agrees with Old	New Narrative More Favorable to Master	New Narrative Less Favorable to Master
Food	21	5	0
Cruelty	23	1	7
Attitude toward master	34	7	7
Master's actions at end of war	23	3	2

Table D.7   Agreement or Disagreement on Important Items of Information

Item	Agreement	Substantial Disagreement or New Information Not Furnished Before
Birthdate	48	13
Parents' occupations	17	9
Occupation as slaves	38	6
Number of marriages	33	1
Belief in haunts	6	1
Occupation in freedom	36	1

Notes

Introduction

1. George P. Rawick, ed., *The American Slave*. For another valuable collection of slave narratives, primarily earlier accounts, see John W. Blassingame, ed., *Slave Testimony*.

2. Rawick, *American Slave*, 19:iii, 18:iv.

3. Norman R. Yetman, "The Background of the Slave Narrative Collection." Officials at Southern University's Archives never responded to inquiries from this author about the Cade collection, and other researchers have encountered the same lack of response.

4. Rawick, *American Slave*, 1:xvii.

5. Charles L. Perdue, Jr., Thomas E. Barden, and Robert K. Phillips, eds., *Weevils in the Wheat*.

6. For the text of this memorandum, see Rawick, *American Slave*, 1:173–78.

7. Ulrich Bonnell Phillips, *American Negro Slavery*, p. viii.

8. K. Warner Schaie, "Translations in Gerontology—From Lab to Life: Intellectual Functioning"; Lissy F. Jarvik and Arthur Falek, "Intellectual Stability and Survival in the Aged"; Robert L. Kahn, Steven H. Zarit, Nancy M. Hilbert, and George Niederehe, "Memory Complaint and Impairment in the Aged"; June E. Blum, Edward T. Clark, and Lissy F. Jarvik, "The New York State Psychiatric Institute Study of Aging Twins," pp. 13–20.

9. Perdue, Barden, and Phillips, *Weevils in the Wheat*, pp. 205, 219–20; Rawick, *American Slave*, 4:part II, 189; 2:part II, 298.

10. Rawick, *American Slave*, 7:Oklahoma, 206.

11. Ibid., 4:part I, 134; 2:part II, 196.

12. A handful of interviews were either too short or too poor in quality to yield useful information.

13. C. Vann Woodward, "History From Slave Sources," pp. 470–81.

14. Ibid., p. 480.

Chapter 1

1. Eugene D. Genovese, *Roll, Jordan, Roll*, pp. 3, 74.
2. George P. Rawick, ed., *The American Slave*, 7:Oklahoma, 308; 11:Missouri, 338.
3. Ibid., 2:part I, 6; 13:part III, 258; 6:Alabama, 358.
4. Ibid., 3:part III, 284–85; 11:part VII, 52; 4:82–83; 5:part III, 139; 4:part II, 127–28.
5. Ibid., 12:part II, 330, 247; 7:Oklahoma, 94.
6. Ibid., 13:part IV, 198; Charles L. Perdue, Jr., Thomas E. Barden, and Robert K. Phillips, eds., *Weevils in the Wheat*, p. 167; Rawick, *American Slave*, 14:250.
7. Rawick, *American Slave*, 16:Virginia, 11; Perdue, Barden, and Phillips, *Weevils in the Wheat*, p. 258.
8. Rawick, *American Slave*, 18:253.
9. Ibid., 12:part II, 107; 4:part I, 1; 5:part IV, 129.
10. Ibid., 13:part III, 48; 6:Alabama, 273; 12:part I, 347.
11. Ibid., 4:part I, 237; 5:part IV, 188; 6:Alabama, 258; 5:part III, 223.
12. Ibid., 5:part IV, 122, 71; 4:part II, 63, 68–69.
13. Ibid., 14:118, 286–87; 6:Indiana, 126.
14. Frederick Law Olmsted, *The Slave States*, p. 73.
15. Kenneth M. Stampp, *The Peculiar Institution*, pp. 30–31.
16. Rawick, *American Slave*, 12:part I, 198; 12:part II, 227; 5:part III, 210; 5:part IV, 125; 6:Alabama, 334.
17. Ibid., 7:Oklahoma, 132; 18:134; 7:Oklahoma, 89; 6:Alabama, 132; 5:part IV, 212.
18. Ibid., 6:Alabama, 28.
19. Ibid., 17:129; 12:part I, 110; 2:part I, 293; Perdue, Barden, and Phillips, *Weevils in the Wheat*, p. 130. For some valuable insights into the development of slave children, the author wishes to thank one of his former students, Mr. Fletcher McIlwain, who wrote his senior honors paper on the socialization of the slave child.
20. Rawick, *American Slave*, 18:114.
21. Ibid., 9:part IV, 254, 7:Mississippi, 12; 7:Oklahoma, 227–28; 7:Mississippi, 138–39; 8:part II, 265–66; 11:Missouri, 1–2; 9:part III, 283.
22. Perdue, Barden, and Phillips, *Weevils in the Wheat*, p. 62; Rawick, *American Slave*, 16:Virginia, 51.
23. Rawick, *American Slave*, 2:part II, 197–98; 7:Oklahoma, 270–71; 2:part II, 235, 329.
24. Ibid., 18:187; 2:part I, 151.

Chapter 2

1. George P. Rawick, ed., *The American Slave*, 4:part I, 278; 2:part II, 281; 4:part II, 180; 6:Alabama, 129.

2. Ibid., 13:part IV, 104, 181–82.

3. Ibid., 154; 5:part IV, 16. These descriptions do not preclude the possibility that some slaves' diet was nutritionally inadequate. See Kenneth F. Kiple and Virginia H. Kiple, "Black Tongue and Black Men," and Leslie Howard Owens, *This Species of Property*, chap. 3.

4. Ibid., 6:Indiana, 73; 5:part III, 259; 6:Alabama, 306.

5. Ibid., 5:part III, 259; 6:Alabama, 417; 12:part II, 5; 6:Alabama, 393; 7:Oklahoma, 74; 2:part I, 192; 6:Indiana, 115; 4:part I, 71; 10:part V, 157; 12:part II, 131.

6. Ibid., 13:part IV, 297; 5:part IV, 27–29; Charles L. Perdue, Jr., Thomas E. Barden, and Robert K. Phillips, eds., *Weevils in the Wheat*, p. 206; Rawick, *American Slave*, 6:Alabama, 432; 5:part IV, 80–81.

7. Rawick, *American Slave*, 2:part II, 139–40; 3:part IV, 117–18; 10:part V, 347–48; 2:part I, 338; 5:part IV, 78.

8. Sidney Andrews, *The South Since the War*, pp. 25–26.

9. Rawick, *American Slave*, 2:part II, 57, 9:part IV, 9–19.

10. Ibid., 14:396; 3:part III, 260; 9:part IV, 9–19; 2:part II, 101; 13:part IV, 202, 218; 6:Indiana, 74, 200; 2:part II, 235.

11. Ibid., 9:part III, 96.

12. Ibid., 10:part V, 197; 5:part IV, 176–78; 17:127; 10:part VI, 223; 5:part IV, 138; 5:part III, 6; 5:part II, 237; 16:Kentucky, 34; 4:part I, 158; 5:part III, 44; 5:part IV, 189; Perdue, Barden, and Phillips, *Weevils in the Wheat*, p. 209; Rawick, *American Slave*, 14:30–31.

13. Mary Boykin Chesnut, *A Diary from Dixie*, pp. 21, 122, 434–35; Rawick, *American Slave*, 15:97; 18:2.

14. Ibid., 15:9; 6:Alabama, 58–61; 4:part II, 253.

15. Ibid., 10:part V, 353; 6:Alabama, 428; 13:part IV, 22; 9:part III, 328; 14:384; Perdue, Barden, and Phillips, *Weevils in the Wheat*, p. 327.

16. Rawick, *American Slave*, 7:Mississippi, 61–62; 5:part IV, 41; 4:part I, 302; 6:Indiana, 99.

17. Ibid., 12:part II, 239; 13:part III, 48–50; 10:part VI, 140.

18. Ibid., 4:part I, 225.

19. Ibid., 19:156; John W. Blassingame, *The Slave Community*, pp. 85–86; Rawick, *American Slave*, 3:part III, 167–68; Herbert G. Gutman, *The Black Family in Slavery and Freedom*, pp. 88–93; Rawick, *American Slave*, 2:part I, 208.

20. Rawick, *American Slave*, 3:part III, 167–68; 2:part I, 231; 6:Indiana, 128; Perdue, Barden, and Phillips, *Weevils in the Wheat*, p. 49; Rawick, *American Slave*, 9:part IV, 192; 2:part I, 39; 3:part IV, 43.

21. Rawick, *American Slave*, 18:42, 156, 138.

22. Ibid., 5:part III, 18; 6:Indiana, 139; 2:part I, 208; 12:part I, 207; 12:part II, 296.

23. The statistic gamma measures the degree of association between two variables that are on ordinal scales. Its value varies between −1 and +1; the greater the absolute value of gamma, the greater the degree of association.

24. Ibid., 13:part III, 97; 2:part I, 52; 4:part I, 302–4.

25. Ibid., 3:part IV, 148; 2:part I, 225; 4:part I, 75; 13:part IV, 135.

26. Ibid., 3:part IV, 2; 2:part I, 245–46; 4:part II, 178; 4:part I, 205.

27. Ibid., 13:part III, 67, 58, 89; 18:9.

28. Yule's Q, which varies beteen zero and one, measures the degree of association between two dichotomous variables and is computed by dividing the difference of the products of the diagonals (in the matrix) by the sum of the products of the diagonals.

29. Perdue, Barden, and Phillips, *Weevils in the Wheat*, p. 122; Rawick, *American Slave*, 13:part IV, 196; 17:356.

30. Rawick, *American Slave*, 4:part I, 267; 16:Tennessee, 80; 9:part III, 127; 7:Mississippi, 130; 6:Indiana, 158–61; 18:134, 140; 5:part IV, 110; 8:part II, 316; 6:Indiana, 98.

31. Ibid., 8:part I, 71; 6:Indiana, 167–68; Perdue, Barden, and Phillips, *Weevils in the Wheat*, p. 210; Rawick, *American Slave*, 18:76, 221.

32. Perdue, Barden, and Phillips, *Weevils in the Wheat*, pp. 55–56; Rawick, *American Slave*, 15:part II, 199–201.

33. Rawick, *American Slave*, 8:part II, 326; 3:part III, 152–53; 8:part I, 36; 4:part I, 303.

34. Ibid., 13:part III, 183; 6:Indiana, 157; 6:Alabama, 220; 14:84.

35. Perdue, Barden, and Phillips, *Weevils in the Wheat,* p. 290; Rawick, *American Slave*, 2:part II, 166; 13:part IV, 357.

36. Rawick, *American Slave*, 3:part III, 49; 6:Alabama, 66; 5:part III, 238; 4:part I, 192–93; 6:Alabama, 52–53, 66, 2; 14:part I, 14; 2:part II, 49; 7:Oklahoma, 216.

37. Ibid., 7:Oklahoma, 50; 11:Missouri, 343; 12:part II, 29, 51, 240; 13:part III, 187; 12:part I, 186; 4:part II, 43, 46.

38. Ibid., 3:part III, 168–69; 3:part IV, 171; 3:part III, 233–34; 7:Oklahoma, 112; 6:Alabama, 106; 15:345; 5:part IV, 101; Supplement, Series 1, 9:1705; 7:Oklahoma, 66–67.

Chapter 3

1. George P. Rawick, ed., *The American Slave*, 6:Indiana, 78; 5:part IV, 204; 6:Alabama, 3; 10:part VI, 353; 8:part II, 17; 7:Oklahoma, 326.
2. Ibid., 7:Oklahoma, 113; 7:Mississippi, 38.
3. Frederick Law Olmsted, *The Slave States*, p. 71; Rawick, *American Slave*, 3:part III, 92.
4. Rawick, *American Slave*, 8:part II, 13; 7:Mississippi, 171; 5:part III, 5–6; 6:Alabama, 417.
5. Ibid., 7:Oklahoma, 239; 4:part I, 203.
6. Charles L. Perdue, Jr., Thomas E. Barden, and Robert K. Phillips, eds., *Weevils in the Wheat*, pp. IV, 181–83.
7. Rawick, *American Slave*, 5:part III, 11; 17:98; 4:part I, 11; 5:part III, 133; 4:part II, 116; 13:part IV, 192.
8. Ibid., 2:part I, 2; 18:9.
9. Ibid., 14:424; 18:137–38; 11:Arkansas, part VII, 174; 9:part III, 162; 12:part I, 302; 4:part II, 181; 5:part IV, 75; 4:part I, 198; 8:part II, 259; 11:Missouri, 108; 19:216; 14:60.
10. Ibid., 12:part II, 59; 13:part III, 186–87.
11. Ibid., 5:part IV, 68; 13:part IV, 182, 195; Olmsted, *Slave States*, p. 86.
12. Rawick, *American Slave*, 13:part III, 240, 287, 213; 2:part II, 97; 14:153; Perdue, Barden, and Phillips, *Weevils in the Wheat*, p. 181.
13. Rawick, *American Slave*, 2:part II, 145; 15:132; 7:Oklahoma, 17.
14. Ibid., 5:part III, 132–37.
15. Ibid., 5:part III, 46.
16. Ibid., 11:Missouri, 332; 12:part II, 235.
17. Ibid., 9:part IV, 108; 13: part III, 91–103; 2:part II, 36.
18. Ibid., 12:part II, 187; 7:Oklahoma, 317; 16:Ohio, 98.
19. Ibid., 18:254; 13:part IV, 182.
20. Ibid., 5:part IV, 41; 3:part IV, 113; 7:Mississippi, 51; 12:part II, 14; Perdue, Barden, and Phillips, *Weevils in the Wheat*, p. 125; Rawick, *American Slave*, 12:part I, 198–99; 5:part III, 248.
21. Rawick, *American Slave*, 2:part II, 236–37; 4:part I, 138–39; 8:part II, 42; 7:Oklahoma, 160; 18:2.
22. Ibid., 13:part IV, 182; 13:part III, 5–6; 6:Alabama, 283.
23. Ibid., 7:Oklahoma, 135; 11:Missouri, 170; 18:116; 5:part IV, 129, 145; 4:part I, 122.
24. Ibid., 2:part II, 65–66.
25. Ibid., 7:Oklahoma, 74, 27; 7:Mississippi, 12; 16:Maryland, 40; 9:part IV, 253; 7:Oklahoma, 346.

Chapter 4

1. George P. Rawick, ed., *The American Slave*, 10:part V, 315; 6:Indiana, 193.
2. Eugene D. Genovese, *Roll, Jordan, Roll*, pp. 3–4.
3. Frederick Law Olmsted, *The Slave States*, pp. 209–10, Mary Boykin Chesnut, *A Diary from Dixie*, pp. 144, 163, 433, 199–200.
4. Rawick, *American Slave*, 5:part III, 83; 4:part I, 296; 4:part II, 8; 4:part I, 279–80.
5. Ibid., 14:362; 18:161; 16:Virginia, 50: Charles L. Perdue, Jr., Thomas E. Barden, and Robert K. Phillips, eds., *Weevils in the Wheat*, p. 128; Rawick, *American Slave*, 7:Oklahoma, 210.
6. Rawick, *American Slave*, 10:part V, 5; 13:part III, 113; 10:part VI, 165; 2:part I, 16.
7. Perdue, Barden, and Phillips, *Weevils in the Wheat*, pp. 220, 235.
8. Ibid., pp. 54–55, 214.
9. Rawick, *American Slave*, 2:part II, 62; Olmsted, *Slave States*, pp. 92, 177; Judith Wragg Chase, *Afro-American Art and Craft*, pp. 52–53.
10. Rawick, *American Slave*, 5:part IV, 198; John W. Blassingame, *The Slave Community*, pp. 32, 34–35.
11. Charles Stearns, *The Black Man of the South and the Rebels*, pp. 371–72.
12. Rawick, *American Slave*, 2:part I, 2.
13. Ibid., 5:part IV, 39, 46, 86–88.
14. Ibid., 5:part IV, 46; 7:Oklahoma, 15; 19:208; 2:part I, 164–65.
15. John S. Mbiti, *African Religions and Philosophy*, p. 83; Rawick, *American Slave*, 13:part IV, 173; 2:part I, 334; 6:Alabama, 186.
16. Rawick, *American Slave*, 2:part I, 47; 19:48, 50, 90.
17. Ibid., 4:part II, 3; 5:part IV, 259; 4:part II, 3–4; 5:part IV, 261; see also 5:part III, 142–44 and 13:part IV, 270–81.
18. Ibid., 4:part II, 64–65; 5:part III, 276; 4:part II, 3; 5:part IV, 252–53; 13:part IV, 271.
19. Ibid., 6:Alabama, 322; 7:Oklahoma, 126; 13:part III, 223.
20. Ibid., 4:part II, 294–95; 5:part III, 161; 2:part I, 2–3; 18:100.
21. Ibid., 12:part I, 89; Perdue, Barden, and Phillips, *Weevils in the Wheat*, p. 267.
22. Rawick, *American Slave*, 2:part I, 171; 13:part IV, 285–89, 95.
23. Ibid., 4:part I, 244; 12:part II, 45; 2:part I, 24; 6:Alabama, 235.
24. Rawick, *From Sundown to Sunup*, pp. 39–43.
25. Ibid., 15:157; 2:part I, 316; 3:part III, 130–31; 13:part III, 270; 17:282–83; 13:part III, 200.
26. Ibid., 16:Tennessee, 49; 4:part I, 177; 17:142; 10:part VI, 236; 12:part I, 174; 11:Missouri, 295.

27. Ibid., 2:part II, 111; 5:part III, 69; 4:part II, 6–7; 5:part IV, 43, 198; 11:Missouri, 305; 12:part II, 24–26.

28. Ibid., 18:259; 15: 130; 6:Alabama, 362.

29. Ibid., 16:Tenneessee, 49.

30. Ibid., 12:part I, 330; 16:Virginia, 12, 10; 16:Tennessee, 16; 12:part II, 25.

31. Ibid., 2:part II, 135; 4:part I, 198–99; 4:part I, 266–67, 282; 4:part II, 294; 5:part IV, 86; 6:Alabama, 40.

32. Ibid., 4:part I, 135; 6:Alabama, 398; 12:part II, 131; 7:Oklahoma, 69.

33. Stearns, *Black Man of the South*, p. 347; Rawick, *American Slave*, 12:part II, 131.

34. Rawick, *American Slave*, 11:part VII, 174; 12:part I, 302; 4:part II, 181; 8:part II, 259.

35. Ibid., 13:part IV, 319.

36. Ibid., 13:part IV, 201; 18:259; 4:part II, 9; 16:Tennessee, 45.

37. Ibid., 17:214.

Chapter 5

1. George P. Rawick, ed., *The American Slave*, 5:part III, 204; *The War of the Rebellion*, Series 1, 47:part II, 40.

2. Rawick, *American Slave*, 18:4; 5:part IV, 205; 14:161–62.

3. Ibid., 9:part III, 78.

4. Bell Irvin Wiley, *Southern Negroes, 1861–1865*; Charles L. Perdue, Jr., Thomas E. Barden, and Robert K. Phillips, eds., *Weevils in the Wheat*, p. 292.

5. Mrs. Irby Morgan, *How It Was*, pp. 112–15, 145.

6. Rawick, *American Slave*, 14:88.

7. Ibid., 3:part III, 26; 2:part II, 217; 8:part I, 118; 2:part I, 43, 149–51; 5:part IV, 141–43.

8. Ibid., 14:459; 3:part III, 3.

9. Ibid., 14:97, 455; 11:part VII, 240.

10. Ibid., 8:part I, 41; 13:part III, 68; 12:part II, 28–30; 13:part IV, 130–31; *War of the Rebellion*, Series 1, 32:part II, 477; Robert Manson Myers, ed., *The Children of Pride*, 1229; *War of the Rebellion*, Series 1, 47:part II, 37. Major General George Halleck was also aware of the slaves' distrust of the federal army. See *War of the Rebellion*, Series 1, 44:840.

11. Rawick, *American Slave*, 9:part IV, 244–45; 13:part III, 343, 196, 162; 13:part IV, 228.

12. Perdue, Barden, and Phillips, *Weevils in the Wheat*, p. 159;

Rawick, *American Slave*, 6:Alabama, 216–17; 3:part III, 170; Perdue, Barden, and Phillips, *Weevils in the Wheat*, p. 121.

13. Rawick, *American Slave*, 3:part IV, 239; 7:Oklahoma, 358; 10:part V, 185.

14. Ibid., 7:Oklahoma, 281; 12:part II, 262–63, 278–79; 14:68.

15. Ibid., 5:part III, 267; Perdue, Barden, and Phillips, *Weevils in the Wheat*, pp. 58–59, 234.

16. Perdue, Barden, and Phillips, *Weevils in the Wheat*, p. 180.

17. Rawick, *American Slave*, 12:part II, 70–71; 14:62; 3:part III, 49.

18. Ibid., 14:145; 18:133.

19. Ibid., 4:part II, 189; 10:part V, 286.

20. Ibid., 7:Mississippi, 16.

21. Ibid., 4:part I, 209; 5:part III, 70.

22. Ibid., 13:part III, 242; 5:part III, 78; 9:part IV, 26; 5:part III, 70; *War of the Rebellion*, Series 1, 49:part II, 1041.

23. Rawick, *American Slave*, 12:part II, 236; 13:part III, 204; *War of the Rebellion*, Series 1, 49:part II, 1041, 1068; Robert Preston Brooks, *The Agrarian Revolution in Georgia, 1865–1912*, pp. 13–14; Rawick, *American Slave*, 8:part II, 261. Many slaves west of the Mississippi River also reported that their emancipation did not come until 19 June 1865, when the United States Army made freedom official. For examples, see Rawick, *American Slave*, 9:part III, 156, 164; 7:Oklahoma, 106.

24. Rawick, *American Slave*, 7:Oklahoma, 167; 5:part IV, 124; 2:part I, 119; 13:part IV, 203; 12:part II, 236, 133; *War of the Rebellion*, Series 1, 47:part II, 40.

25. Perdue, Barden, and Phillips, *Weevils in the Wheat*, p. 64; Rawick, *American Slave*, 5:part III, 83–84; 12:part II, 218; 7:Mississippi, 168.

26. James L. Roark, *Masters Without Slaves*.

27. Rawick, *American Slave*, 3:part IV, 27; 7:Oklahoma, 276; 5:part III, 258–61; 17:130; 5:part IV, 133; 4:part II, 146; 4:part I, 47; 12:part II, 133.

28. Ibid., 7:Mississippi, 132; 5:part IV, 154; 14:215; 17:239; 4:part I, 122; 6:Alabama, 231.

29. Ibid., 13:part IV, 166.

30. Ibid., 4:part I, 247; 10:part VI, 163; Perdue, Barden and Phillips, *Weevils in the Wheat*, p. 89.

31. See chap. 2, n. 23.

32. Rawick, *American Slave*, 4:part II, 133; 5:part III, 204.

Chapter 6

1. George P. Rawick, ed., *The American Slave*, 4:part I, 264; 14:252; 7:Oklahoma, 231; 11:Missouri, 114–15.

2. Ibid., 13:part III, 176; 11:Missouri, 192; 12:part I, 351; 6:Indiana, 5.

3. Ibid., 5:part IV, 82; 17:215, 209–10; 10:part V, 182; 8:part II, 6; 10: part V, 27–28, 124. See also Todd L. Savitt, "The Medical Department of the Freedmen's Bureau in Georgia."

4. The difference between table 6.1 and this figure of 85 percent arises from two factors: most farm-to-town migrations probably were within the same state, and a larger number of former slaves supplied information on their state of residence than supplied information on the distance of their migration.

5. Rawick, *American Slave*, 15:268; 5:part III, 26; 4:part II, 171; 8:part II, 6; 7:Oklahoma, 18.

6. Ibid., 11:part VII, 253; 11:Missouri, 146; 16:Tennessee, 43–44; 13:part IV, 3; 11:Missouri, 268; 16:Kentucky, 53; 17:226–27.

7. Charles L. Perdue, Jr., Thomas E. Barden, and Robert K. Phillips, eds., *Weevils in the Wheat*, p. 213; Rawick, *American Slave*, 2:part I, 219; 15:334, 86; 14:205.

8. Rawick, *American Slave*, 2:part I, 241; 6:Indiana, 209; 3:part III, 173.

9. Ibid., 5:part III, 176; 10:part VI, 229; 8:part I, 139; 16:Virginia, 56.

10. Ibid., 5:part IV, 148–49; 5:part III, 235.

11. Ibid., 8:part II, 106; 4:part II, 108; 4:part I, 222; 2:part II, 39; Robert Manson Myers, ed., *The Children of Pride*, pp. 1308–9; Rawick, *American Slave*, 4:part I, 300; 6:Alabama, 218; 2:part I, 243; 5:part III, 112; 7:Mississippi, 132, 140–41, 147; 9:part III, 363; 15:part II, 201; 7:Mississippi, 103; 5:part IV, 114; Perdue, Barden, and Phillips, *Weevils in the Wheat*, p. 72.

12. Rawick, *American Slave*, 11:Missouri, 351; 13:part III, 204; 12:part II, 330–33; 17:36; 6:Indiana, 123. See also Peter Kolchin, *First Freedom*, chap. 1 and pp. 35–46.

13. Rawick, *American Slave*, 11:Missouri, 315; 4:part I, 285–88; 3:part III, 165; 10:part VI, 195; 10:part VI, 77–78.

14. Ibid., 3:part IV, 238; 5:part III, 123; 3:part IV, 159; 9:part III, 392; 2:part I, 78.

15. Ibid., 2:part I, 177; 2:part II, 27.

16. Ibid., 5:part IV, 98; 4:part I, 3; 2:part I, 31, 34, 35, 15; 3:part III, 155; 2:part I, 170.

17. Ibid., 7:Mississippi, 42; 3:part III, 178; 3:part IV, 204; 7:Mississippi, 64; 3:part III, 228; 8:part I, 54.

18. Ibid., 8:part I, 81; Gladys-Marie Fry, *Night Riders in Black Folk History*, pp. 117–21; Rawick, *American Slave*, 17:200; 9:part III, 173.

19. Rawick, *American Slave*, 4:part I, 38; 3:part IV, 159, 43, 37; 8:part II, 107; 7:Mississippi, 173.

20. Ibid., 11:part VII, 97, 98; 8:part II, 145–46; 5:part IV, 142; 4:part I, 187a; 4:part II, 30–31; 10:part VI, 130; 7:Oklahoma, 143; 7:Mississippi, 16; 6:Indiana, 129–30; 12:part I, 351; 13:part III, 163; 16:Ohio, 31; 5:part III, 137; 6:Alabama, 218–19; 8:part I, 58. See also 4:part II, 112 and 8:part I, 2.

21. Ibid., 2:part I, 40–41; 5:part IV, 90; 6:Indiana, 136; 5:part III, 155; 9:part III, 363; 6:Alabama, 421; 4:part II, 176; 9:part IV, 294; 10:part VI, 241–42.

22. Ibid., 12:part I, 193; 2:part II, 121; 8:part I, 208; 7:Mississippi, 9; 5: part III, 186–97; 4:part II, 112.

23. Ibid., 7:Mississippi, 54.

24. Ibid., 3:part II, 128–29.

Chapter 7

1. George P. Rawick, ed., *The American Slave*, 14:361, 236.

2. Ibid., 7:Mississippi, 94–97; 15:122–23.

3. Ibid., 6:Indiana, 207; 8:part I, 78; 9:part IV, 174.

4. Ibid., 2:part I, 78; 5:part III, 261; 11:Missouri, 81–82.

5. Ibid., 5:part IV, 65, 70, 137.

6. Ibid., 3:part IV, 173; 5:part IV, 117; 12:part II, 36.

7. Perhaps the best succinct description of this system is in V. O. Key, Jr., *Southern Politics*, chap. 1.

8. I gratefully credit my colleague, Lyman Johnson, for this idea, which he forcefully presented to me in one of our discussions. See also Rawick, *American Slave*, Supplement, Series 1, 10:2225; 5:475.

9. Rawick, *American Slave*, 14:2; Charles L. Perdue, Jr., Thomas E. Barden, and Robert K. Phillips, *Weevils in the Wheat*, p. 124. Rawick, *American Slave*, 9:part III, 128; Forrest McDonald and Grady McWhinney, "The Antebellum Southern Herdsman," p. 165.

10. Rawick, *American Slave*, 10:part VI, 281; 2:part II, 35; 3:part IV, 47.

11. Ibid., 2:part II, 38; 2:part I, 305; 2:part II, 41.

12. Ibid., 5:part III, 179; 2:part I, 236; 2:part II, 178.

13. Ibid., 3:part IV, 173; 11:Missouri, 198.

14. Ibid., 10:part V, 296; 12:part II, 36.

15. Ibid., 2:part I, 36; 4:part II, 122; 13:part IV, 105.
16. Ibid., 2:part II, 222; 10:part V, 312; 15:358.
17. Ibid., 5:part III, 112; 10:part VI, 197.
18. Ibid., 4:part II, 168; 4:part I, 287; 2:part I, 302; 7:Oklahoma, 215; 4:part I, 192.
19. Ibid., 2:part I, 39; 4:part I, 117; 5:part III, 270–73.
20. Ibid., 4:part II, 129; 4:part I, 153; 3:part III, 16; 4:part II, 204; 2:part I, 248, 335; 2:part II, 137; 13:part III, 102.
21. Ibid., 8:part I, 12; 5:part IV, 40; 10:part VI, 285; 2:part I, 100; 4:part II, 114.

Bibliography

Andrews, Sidney. *The South Since the War, as Shown by Fourteen Weeks of Travel and Observation in Georgia and the Carolinas*. Boston: Ticknor and Fields, 1866.

Blassingame, John W. *The Slave Community: Plantation Life in the Antebellum South*. New York: Oxford University Press, 1972.

————. "Using the Testimony of Ex-Slaves: Approaches and Problems." *Journal of Southern History* 41 (1975):473–92.

————, ed. *Slave Testimony: Two Centuries of Letters, Speeches, Interviews, and Autobiographies*. Baton Rouge: Louisiana State University Press, 1977.

Blum, June E.; Clark, Edward T.; and Jarvik, Lissy F. "The New York State Psychiatric Institute Study of Aging Twins." *Intellectual Functioning in Adults*. Edited by Lissy F. Jarvik, Carl Eisdorfer, and June E. Blum. New York: Springer Publishing Co., 1973.

Botkin, B. A., ed. *Lay My Burden Down: A Folk History of Slavery*. Chicago: University of Chicago Press, 1945.

————. "The Slave as His Own Interpreter." *Library of Congress Quarterly Journal of Current Acquisitions* 2 (1944):37–63.

Brooks, Robert Preston. *The Agrarian Revolution in Georgia, 1865–1912*. Bulletin of the University of Wisconsin, no. 639, History Series, vol. 3, no. 3.

Cade, John B. "Out of the Mouths of Ex-Slaves." *Journal of Negro History* 20 (1935):294–337.

Chase, Judith Wragg. *Afro-American Art and Craft*. New York: Van Nostrand-Reinhold Co., 1971.

Chesnut, Mary Boykin. *A Diary from Dixie*. Edited by Ben Ames Williams. Boston: Houghton Mifflin Co., 1949.

Davis, David Brion. "Slavery and the Post-World War II Historians." *Daedalus* 103 (1974):1–16.

Fry, Gladys-Marie. *Night Riders in Black Folk History*. Knoxville: University of Tennessee Press, 1975.

Bibliography

Genovese, Eugene D. "Getting to Know the Slaves." *New York Review of Books*, 21 September 1972, pp. 16–19.

————. *Roll, Jordan, Roll: The World the Slaves Made*. New York: Pantheon Books, 1974.

Gutman, Herbert G. *The Black Family in Slavery and Freedom, 1750–1925*. New York: Pantheon Books, 1976.

Jarvik, Lissy F., and Falek, Arthur. "Intellectual Stability and Survival in the Aged." *Journal of Gerontology* 18 (1963):173–76.

Kahn, Robert L.; Zarit, Steven H.; Hilbert, Nancy M.; and Niederehe, George. "Memory Complaint and Impairment in the Aged." *Archives of General Psychiatry* 32 (1975):1569–73.

Key, V. O., Jr., with the assistance of Heard, Alexander. *Southern Politics in State and Nation*. New York: Alfred A. Knopf, 1949.

Kiple, Kenneth F., and Kiple, Virginia H. "Black Tongue and Black Men: Pellagra and Slavery in the Antebellum South." *Journal of Southern History* 43 (1977):411–28.

Kolchin, Peter. *First Freedom: The Responses of Alabama's Blacks to Emancipation and Reconstruction*. Contributions in American History, no. 20. Westport, Connecticut: Greenwood Press, 1972.

Mbiti, John S. *African Religions and Philosophy*. New York: Frederick A. Praeger, 1969.

McDonald, Forrest, and McWhiney, Grady. "The Antebellum Southern Herdsman: A Reinterpretation." *Journal of Southern History* 41 (1975):147–66.

Morgan, Mrs. Irby. *How It Was: Four Years Among the Rebels*. Nashville: Publishing House of the Methodist Episcopal Church South, 1892.

Myers, Robert Manson, ed. *The Children of Pride*. New Haven: Yale University Press, 1972.

Olmsted, Frederick Law. *The Slave States Before the Civil War*. Edited by Harvey Wish. New York: G. P. Putnam's Sons, Capricorn Books, 1959.

Owens, Leslie Howard. *This Species of Property: Slave Life and Culture in the Old South*. New York: Oxford University Press, 1976.

Perdue, Charles L., Jr.; Barden, Thomas E.; and Phillips, Robert K., eds. *Weevils in the Wheat: Interviews with Virginia Ex-Slaves*. Charlottesville: University Press of Virginia, 1976.

Phillips, Ulrich Bonnell. *American Negro Slavery*. New York: D. Appleton-Century Co., 1940.

Rawick, George P., ed. *The American Slave: A Composite Autobiography*. Contributions in Afro-American and African Studies, no. 11. 19 vols. Series 1. Vol. 1, *From Sundown to Sunup: The Making of the Black Community*, by George P. Rawick. Vol. 2, *South Carolina Narratives*,

Parts I and II. Vol. 3, *South Carolina Narratives, Parts III and IV.* Vol. 4, *Texas Narratives, Parts I and II.* Vol. 5, *Texas Narratives, Parts III and IV.* Vol. 6, *Alabama and Indiana Narratives.* Vol. 7, *Oklahoma and Mississippi Narratives.* Series 2. Vol. 8, *Arkansas Narratives, Parts I and II.* Vol. 9, *Arkansas Narratives, Parts III and IV.* Vol. 10, *Arkansas Narratives, Parts V and VI.* Vol. 11, *Arkansas Narratives, Part VII, and Missouri Narratives.* Vol. 12, *Georgia Narratives, Parts I and II.* Vol. 13, *Georgia Narratives, Parts III and IV.* Vol. 14, *North Carolina Narratives, Part I.* Vol. 15, *North Carolina Narratives, Part II.* Vol. 16, *Kansas, Kentucky, Maryland, Ohio, Virginia, and Tennessee Narratives.* Vol. 17, *Florida Narratives.* Vol. 18, *Unwritten History of Slavery (Fisk University).* Vol. 19, *God Struck Me Dead (Fisk University).* Westport, Connecticut: Greenwood Publishing Company, 1972.

———. *The American Slave: A Composite Autobiography.* Contributions in Afro-American and African Studies, no. 35. 12 vols. Supplement, Series 1. Vol. 1, *Alabama Narratives.* Vol. 2, *Arkansas, Colorado, Minnesota, Missouri and Oregon and Washington Narratives.* Vol. 3, *Georgia Narratives, Part I.* Vol. 4, *Georgia Narratives, Part II.* Vol. 5, *Indiana and Ohio Narratives.* Vol. 6, *Mississippi Narratives, Part I.* Vol. 7, *Mississippi Narratives, Part II.* Vol. 8, *Mississippi Narratives, Part III.* Vol. 9, *Mississippi Narratives, Part IV.* Vol. 10, *Mississippi Narratives, Part V.* Vol. 11, *North Carolina and South Carolina Narratives.* Vol. 12, *Oklahoma Narratives.* Westport, Connecticut: Greenwood Press, 1977.

Roark, James L. *Masters Without Slaves: Southern Planters in the Civil War and Reconstruction.* New York: W. W. Norton and Co., 1977.

Savitt, Todd L. "The Medical Department of the Freedmen's Bureau in Georgia: The First Year." Unpublished paper in author's possession.

Schaie, K. Warner. "Translations in Gerontology—From Lab to Life: Intellectual Functioning." *American Psychologist* 29 (1974):802–7.

Stampp, Kenneth M. *The Peculiar Institution: Slavery in the Ante-Bellum South.* New York: Alfred A. Knopf, 1956.

Stearns, Charles. *The Black Man of the South and the Rebels.* New York: American News Company, 1872.

The War of the Rebellion: A Compilation of the Official Records of the Union and Confederate Armies. 130 vols. Washington: Government Printing Office, 1880–1901.

Wiley, Bell Irvin. *Southern Negroes, 1861–1865.* New Haven: Yale University Press, 1938.

Woodward, C. Vann. "History From Slave Sources." *American Historical Review* 79 (1974):470–81.

Writers Program, Louisiana. *Gumbo Ya-Ya.* Boston: Houghton Mifflin Co., 1945.

Yetman, Norman R. "The Background of the Slave Narrative Collection." *American Quarterly* 19 (1967):534–53.

———, ed. *Voices from Slavery*. New York: Holt, Rinehart and Winston, 1970.

Index